Building the
Innovation School

Building the Innovation School

Infrastructures for Equity in Today's Classrooms

T. Philip Nichols

Foreword by Yasmin B. Kafai

TEACHERS COLLEGE PRESS

TEACHERS COLLEGE | COLUMBIA UNIVERSITY
NEW YORK AND LONDON

Published by Teachers College Press,® 1234 Amsterdam Avenue, New York, NY 10027

Front cover design by adam bohannon design. Textures from royyimzy and Forgem via Adobe Stock.

Library of Congress Cataloging-in-Publication Data

Names: Nichols, T. Philip, author.
Title: Building the innovation school : infrastructures for equity in today's
   classrooms / T. Philip Nichols ; foreword by Yasmin Kafai.
Description: New York : Teachers College Press, 2022. | Includes bibliographical
   references and index.
Identifiers: LCCN 2022004595 (print) | LCCN 2022004596 (ebook) |
   ISBN 9780807766781 (paperback) | ISBN 9780807766798 (hardcover) |
   ISBN 9780807780947 (epub)
Subjects: LCSH: Educational innovations—United States. | Educational change—
   United States. | Education—Effect of technological innovations on—
   United States. | Education—Aims and objectives—United States.
Classification: LCC LB1027 .N494 2022 (print) | LCC LB1027 (ebook) |
   DDC 370.973—dc23/eng/20220302
LC record available at https://lccn.loc.gov/2022004595
LC ebook record available at https://lccn.loc.gov/2022004596

ISBN 978-0-8077-6678-1 (paper)
ISBN 978-0-8077-6679-8 (hardcover)
ISBN 978-0-8077-8094-7 (ebook)

Printed on acid-free paper
Manufactured in the United States of America

Contents

Foreword

Rewriting the Playbook for School Innovation

Far too much has been written about vouchers, charters, and computers as playbooks for school innovation. A leading theme in many of these proposals is one of "disruption of schooling" by giving parents a choice which school their children can attend, changing the curriculum and teaching, or providing computers for students. Implementations of any of these proposals by districts and administrators address critical concerns, but often fall short of sustained success. This book by T. Philip Nichols also falls into this category, but it offers a very different proposal: a "disruption of innovation" counternarrative that has different stakeholders in the local school culture become the agents of change who make adjustments and repairs. He argues that a playbook for school innovation should start from below rather than the top and should focus on repair rather than disruption to address equity, inclusion, and social justice.

In *Building the Innovation School,* Nichols provides a much-needed, nuanced account of what happens when an innovation lands in a school, how it gets picked up, what gets renegotiated, and what emerges unexpectedly. His proposal builds on careful observations collected over multiple years and provides detailed insights into how the process of innovation unfolds from the first time teachers and administrators meet in the school district to lay the foundation for the school, to later years when teachers and students deal with revisiting and developing assignments. Nichols frames the analysis in terms of different infrastructures in which schooling takes place. He focuses not just on the pedagogical infrastructure, in how students' self-directed learning is supported and how teachers' successful appropriation of technologies is connected to previous practices, but also on the spatial infrastructure, in how spaces are reconfigured and emerge in addressing the changes and developments of students' learning needs. Most importantly, the stakeholders—students, teachers, and administrators—are not just the recipients of but also active contributors to the innovation.

If we move away from a model of innovation from the top, we still need to address the issue of who or what gets the ball rolling on introducing larger change. In the book, Nichols reminds us that the very idea of public schooling for the common good is an innovation for which it would be difficult, if not impossible, to garner support these days. Returning to the story in *Building the Innovation School,* I note that the initial proposal had all the marks of a conventional innovation approach from the top with its focus on STEM, maker spaces, and competency building. Here Nichols introduces the idea of identifying "imaginaries" that different stakeholders bring to the table, what they see as valuable and relevant in innovation. These imaginaries about innovation might differ in many aspects, but also overlap in some parts. Acknowledging the overlaps and differences rather than ignoring or erasing them turns out to be the essential hard work for making innovation see the light of the day.

Rewriting the playbook about school innovation from below is a bold proposal that shifts our attention from the promise of the big idea to the realization in the local context. The findings from this book also invite us to rethink the mantra of fidelity of implementation that for far too long has been seen as the hallmark of success. While all of this might tell a less grandiose story about innovation, one that sees the collective rather than the individual at the center of action, this approach is a more feasible and also a "humbler" one, as Nichols so rightfully calls it. There is something very hopeful in the message of this book: Innovation can work, but it requires the care and consideration of all involved to flourish.

—*Yasmin B. Kafai*
University of Pennsylvania

Acknowledgments

This is a book about infrastructure—the subtle, even invisible, supports that create, condition, and sustain the observable world around us. Like the innovations it explores, the book is also the outgrowth of such infrastructures. From research to writing to publishing, every stage of its development has been nurtured by a vast and generous community of mentors, colleagues, and comrades. Being able to thank, in print, even a portion of this collective has been a powerful motivation for seeing the book to completion.

I am grateful, first and foremost, to the principal, teachers, staff, and students at the Innovation School. Their creativity and ingenuity were an inspiration through every phase of this study, and their willingness to open their classrooms, and to wrestle with the meaning of "innovation" alongside me and other members of the research team, was a gift I don't take lightly. May their on-the-ground innovating and their commitment to just and equitable learning be an example to all who encounter them in these pages. This book is for them, and for all the educators and students who, likewise, are already and always innovating from below.

This project began life as a dissertation, and as such, it is indebted to the insights of my doctoral committee at the University of Pennsylvania. It was my advisor and chair, Amy Stornaiuolo, who established the university–school partnership from which this study grew, and many of the most clarifying breakthroughs in the project's design and analysis occurred in dialogue with her—on car or train rides to the school, over tacos on campus park benches, or in frantic bursts of text messages. She, along with my other committee members—Gerald Campano, Vivian Gadsden, Carolyn Marvin, and Brian Street—provided incisive feedback and calming reassurance that not only strengthened the research but also offered a model of caring and ethical mentorship that I continually strive to emulate in my own teaching, advising, and consulting. Little of what appears in these pages does not bear, in some form, the indelible mark of their influence. I am so grateful.

The writing and revising of this manuscript were generously supported by a dissertation fellowship from the National Academy of Education and the Spencer Foundation, as well as course releases and a grant from Baylor University. My writing group in Baylor's Curriculum and Instruction department—Kelly Johnston, Lupita Lang, Kevin Magill, Justina Ogodo, Lakia Scott, Neil Shanks—was integral in providing feedback, accountability, and commiseration along the way. Andrew Shrock's keen editorial eye spared readers from the full brunt of my worst writerly tics (though em dashes and parentheticals still abound—alas!). Many thanks are also due to Emily Spangler and the team at Teachers College Press who shepherded the manuscript to publication; without them, this book would quite literally not exist. I appreciate, too, the text's two anonymous reviewers for their suggestions, critiques, and affirmations.

Portions of the book received valuable feedback from members of the American Educational Research Association, History of Education Society, Literacy Research Association, Society for the Social Studies of Science, the Spencer Foundation, and multiple cohorts in the Instructional Technology module of the University of Pennsylvania's Mid-Career Program in Educational Leadership. Several chapters also include sections that were adapted from previously published materials that appeared in *Teachers College Record* (Chapter 1), *Research in the Teaching of English* (Chapter 2), *Phi Delta Kappan* (Chapter 3), *Journal of Adolescent and Adult Literacy* (Chapter 3), and *Educational Leadership* (Chapter 4). Being in dialogue with coauthors, copresenters, audience members, editors, and peer reviewers through these venues has been a privilege, and the words that appear here have undoubtedly been honed through the insights of such generous readers and readings.

I have also been blessed by an expansive network of brilliant and caring mentors, colleagues, coconspirators, and friends who have shared feedback, exchanged emails, or generally tolerated my streams of thought through different stages of this project: Steve Armandt, Katrina Bartow-Jacobs, Etienne Benson, Brooke Blevins, Jason Brennan, Cassie Brownell, Sarah Burriss, Sophia Chaparro, Kevin Clay, David Cohen, Josh Coleman, Laura Desimone, Ezekiel Dixon-Román, Danielle and Elliot Dunn, Adam Edgerton, Will Edwards, Jason Ellis, Nelson Flores, Antero Garcia, María Paula Ghiso, Leif Gustavson, Kris Gutiérrez, Kathy Hall, Dana and Drew Hamilton, Amber Henry, Glynda Hull, Alex Hyres, Jin-Kyeong Jung, Yasmin Kafai, Kevin Leander, Robert LeBlanc, Karon LeCompte, Kim Lenters, Tim Lewis, Susan Lindee, Cassie Lo, Jackie Lopez, David Low, Deb Lui, Susan Lytle, Rhiannon Maton, Lan Ngo, Dierdre Mayer, Alex and Bethany Monea, Sherea Mosley, Sonita Moss, Katie Pak, Jessica Zacher Pandya, Luci Pangrazio, Nora Peterman, Grace Player, Emily Plummer, Robert Rivera-Amezola, Jennifer Rowsell, Alicia Rusoja, Betsy Rymes, Erica Saldívar-Garcia, Emily Schwab, Julian Sefton-Green, Rachel Skrlac-Lo, Rob Simon, Anna Smith, Emmanuel Tabi, Sandra and Tony Talbert, Ebony Elizabeth Thomas, John Tresch, Fred Turner, José van Dijck, Veena Vasudevan, Diane Waff, Jon Wargo, Audrey Watters, and Jim and Valerie Zeldenrust.

Finally, I thank my family: mom and dad, both innovators and educators in their own ways; Britt and Marshal, my might-as-well-be-siblings; my aunts, uncles, cousins, and grandparents—for your boundless love and support. And most of all, Jena, whose care, encouragement, and counsel were the infrastructures that made finishing this book in the middle of a pandemic not just possible, but joyful; I'm so lucky to be your partner.

Introduction

What Do We Talk About When We Talk About Innovation?

Picture an "innovative" classroom. What images come to your mind? Maybe you imagine a particular look and feel to the room, with rows of desks replaced with modular furniture and flexible space, and no clear front of the class from which a teacher can lecture. Maybe your classroom is filled with the latest technologies, like tablets, personalized learning software, 3D printers, virtual reality headsets, and tools for making, crafting, and designing. Or maybe your imagination goes right to the activities of the classroom—what students are *doing* to learn. Are they expressing themselves through self-selected projects, or demonstrating competency by meeting rigorous academic standards? Are they budding software engineers learning to code, or polymaths working across disciplinary boundaries? Are they exercising entrepreneurship, or exploring issues of social justice?

This isn't an exhaustive list of what might have popped into your head. More than likely, you can envision other forms of "innovative" teaching and learning that weren't mentioned. The point of this thought experiment wasn't to settle on a conclusive catalog of "innovations," but to highlight the range of ideas, devices, and practices that are commonly attached to the term. If you're like me or the teachers and administrators I work with, some of the above visions resonate more with your imagined "innovative" classroom than others. Chances are, if you were to compare your assemblage of "innovative" elements with someone else—a colleague, supervisor, or policymaker—there would be both predictable overlaps and surprising divergences. For as widely used as the term "innovation" is, it doesn't have a singular, stable meaning. It's a flexible label—one that people affix to forms of teaching and learning they like and withhold from those they don't. What is "innovative" to one person could be stale or regressive to another.

The term's flexibility might make it tempting to conclude that "innovation" is just a meaningless buzzword. But this would overlook some important realities about the education landscape today. Schools now face tremendous pressures to accommodate the evolving needs of a world in flux. Mobile and connective technologies have reshaped the daily demands

1

of life and work, raising questions about how education ought to keep pace (Collins & Halverson, 2018). Accelerating wealth inequality has perpetuated the underdevelopment of working-class communities and the public institutions that serve them (Piketty, 2014). Less affluent schools are often left to redress raced and classed disparities in academic achievement with ever fewer resources (Ladson-Billings, 2006). Even more, all these challenges unfold against a backdrop of world-historical happenings like pandemics, climate catastrophes, migrant and refugee crises, transnational movements for racial and economic justice, and the global creep of ethnonationalist and antidemocratic governance (Davis, 2016; A. Taylor, 2019). Under such circumstances, the language of "innovation" is far from meaningless. It offers a real, if imprecise, way to talk about the place and purpose of schooling in relation to these developments, and the aspects of teaching and learning that need reimagining in light of them. We need to hold tight to the potential of innovation because we must continue to be hopeful.

There is a tension, then, in today's conceptions of "educational innovation." The phrase signals a need for imaginative possibilities that are broad and ambitious enough to meet the challenges wrought by technological development, globalization, and inequality. Yet its pliability creates challenges for weighing the appropriateness, effectiveness, or ethical implications of any given innovative possibility. A thriving industry has emerged from out of this incongruity, capitalizing on the need for "innovation." Hardly a week passes without a tech mogul, "edupreneur," TED Talk thought leader, or PAC-backed politician announcing the latest device, app, service, curricular add-on, or organizational strategy that is sure to cure the perennial woes of school systems. These innovations-of-the-day may look different, and they may be delivered through different technologies or aimed at different stakeholders, but they share an underlying promise: to disrupt the routines and rituals of schooling as we know it. Each also assures us that unlike past innovations, *this one* is primed to succeed in making education more efficient, effective, and responsive to the needs of a changing world. These promises colonize education by seizing on the ambiguity of the very idea of educational innovation.

Comforting as it sounds, these promises overlook the long history of educational innovations that made similar claims and then faltered in practice (Cuban, 1986; Watters, 2021). Even more, they fail to acknowledge that innovations are never introduced in isolation, but alongside other innovations, some of which are already embedded in schools. Innovations geared toward supporting college- and career-readiness, for instance, may work against those intended to nurture self-expression or promote lifelong learning. The allure of educational innovations can place educators with limited time and budgets in a difficult position. Choose the wrong innovation, and you could be saddled with a resource-draining "solution" that didn't live up to its promises. Hesitate to choose, and you risk "falling behind" other schools, and appearing outdated to students, parents, and community members. Either outcome can have negative implications for the quality of classroom learning and also for the inequities that are reproduced when cure-alls fall short. In such a fraught position, how are educators to choose which innovations are best? Which ought to be implemented, and which are best ignored?

This book argues that these questions, while reasonable and well-meaning, are the wrong starting point for thinking about innovation in schools. In an environment where everything is marketed as "innovative," the appeal of a dependable strategy for distinguishing the "good" innovations from the "bad" ones makes sense. But by focusing on the merits and drawbacks of individual innovations, this orientation leaves unexamined the wider lure the concept of innovation holds in education, the assumptions it carries in freight, and the work it does in different classroom contexts. This book differs from other books about innovation because it takes up this latter line of inquiry. It doesn't weigh the pros and cons of particular innovations. It doesn't speculate about the future of education or the products needed to navigate it. It isn't even especially interested in defining what innovation *is* as much as it is in understanding what innovation *does*: how it works, for whom, and to what ends. In this way, the questions that guide this book don't lead to quick fixes or one-size-fits-all answers. Instead, they offer meaningful resources for interrogating how we think about innovation, so we might imagine alternate orientations for learning that better serve our students. Specifically, in this book I ask:

- What interests and values shape conceptions of "innovation" in education?
- What are the impacts and implications for teaching, learning, and educational equity when competing ideas about "innovation" are put to work in schools and classrooms?
- How might alternate orientations to "innovation" lead to more sustainable infrastructures for quality teaching and learning, and enable all students to flourish?

THE INNOVATION SCHOOL

The book explores these questions using ethnographic research spanning the opening and first 3 years of operation of The Innovation School (all names are pseudonyms)—an urban, public high school in Philadelphia where I managed a university–school research partnership between 2014 and 2017. Part of its district's experimental "Innovation Network," the school emphasizes principles of "making" and "design" (Kafai et al., 2014; Peppler et al., 2016) and is structured around three interdisciplinary "makerspaces" for media production, community organizing, and STEM. These makerspaces operate as standalone classes and as spaces where students can complete projects for their core content-area courses: humanities, science, and math. Students in the school are issued one-to-one laptops for navigating its asynchronous, inquiry-based curriculum, and are assessed using competencies rather than conventional grades. Importantly, the school is also non-selective, meaning its innovative offerings extend to students who might be excluded from similar programs due to income, geography, enrollment caps, or past academic performance. At the time of this study, its demographics were comparable to those of nearby neighborhood schools; the school's population was 80% African American, 15% Latinx, and all students received free lunch.

The university–school partnership was established by Dr. Amy Stornaiuolo and the school's founding principal, Ben, to explore how the school's commitments to technological and pedagogical innovation, content-area learning, and educational equity might benefit students in its classrooms. From the summer before the school opened to the start of its inaugural cohort's senior year, I served as project manager for the partnership. In this role, I led a team of researchers making daily visits to the school, working closely with administrators, teachers, and students—sometimes as participant observers, other times as cofacilitators, academic tutors, sounding boards for professional planning, and in countless other roles that researchers in partnership-based work are often asked to accommodate (Campano et al., 2016). Throughout this process, we documented and studied the successes and challenges that surfaced as diverse (and, at times, competing) innovations were layered together in the policies and practices of the school.

SITUATING THE STUDY

Of course, I did not arrive at the Innovation School as a blank slate. My research with the partnership was informed by my prior experiences with educational innovation. As a former classroom teacher, I was all too familiar with professional development workshops where consultants and product ambassadors marched out the latest innovations for optimizing instruction. One year, it was Smartboards; the next, a new curriculum adoption; and after that, a learning management system. To varying degrees, these initiatives seemed promising. However, implementing them always surfaced unanticipated frictions—from the mild malfunctioning of new hardware to more severe shifts in the classroom environment that worked against students. Over time, I began to see that what one person considered "innovative" could be an obstacle for another. This raised my interest in how certain innovations came to be privileged and prioritized over others, and how the pressure to keep pace with the latest "innovative" trends could have uneven consequences for those implementing them. These questions stayed with me throughout my work with the partnership.

My research at the Innovation School was also shaped by the local circumstances that led to its opening. The 2 years before the school began were marred by devastating district cuts that shuttered more than 30 neighborhood schools in Philadelphia, mostly in low income, Black communities. Around the city, Head Start programs were privatized, and over 3,700 teachers, counselors, and aides were fired. Sensing parallels to similar austerity measures and policy priorities unfolding in other large urban districts (Buras, 2015; Ewing, 2018), teachers, students, and community activists organized protests to pressure the district for more equitable resource distribution in city schools. In response, the district announced it would open a handful of experimental "innovation schools" to bring technology-rich, inquiry-based learning to students disparately impacted by the cuts and closings. Termed "The Innovation Gamble" by local journalists (Herold, 2013), the district's strategy highlighted a dimension of "innovation" in school reform efforts we discussed above. The concept did not just refer to new devices and pedagogical interventions. Rather, invoking "innovation" was a rhetorical strategy—a way to project legitimacy and dynamism even in the face of upheaval and uncertainty. Against this backdrop, I centered research in the university–school partnership not just on what innovations were being implemented, but also how the concept itself was being mobilized, for whom, and to what ends.

Finally, my work with the Innovation School was informed by my positionality. As a White cisgender man affiliated with an elite private university, my vantage point for studying innovation in a public high school that served mostly students of color was far from neutral. There is a long history of similarly raced, gendered, and institutionally linked scholars who have promoted and studied "innovative" reforms that ultimately worked to entrench racial and economic stratification (Anderson, 1987; Rodney, 1972; K.-Y. Taylor, 2019). Furthermore, among scholars aware of such legacies, there also exists a troubling tendency toward "damage-centered" research (Paris, 2019; Tuck, 2009)—scholarship that, in seeking to spotlight forms of oppression, overlooks the agentive movements of nondominant communities as they work within and against compromised systems. My research in the partnership, then, demanded that I continually examine my place in the "matrix of domination" (Collins, 1990) that allowed injustices (educational and otherwise) to persist, and that privileged insights and interventions "from above" over the creative ingenuity of teachers and students on the ground. Throughout the study, the insights of teachers and students were a source of ongoing reflection in analytic memos, research team meetings, and frank conversations with the educators and students with whom we partnered.

These reflections formed the foundation for the orientation to innovation developed in this book—what I call *innovation from below.*

The Linear Model of Innovation

Before introducing this book's approach to innovation, it will be helpful to set the stage with a closer look at the orientation it is meant to challenge: the *linear model* of innovation. This is the name economists give to the idea of "innovation" that has most decisively shaped the concept's usage in education to date. It is the formal term for the popular belief that innovation is a steady process of continual improvement. It promises disruption and assures success if we are willing to adapt. The model's name derives from the theory that innovations emerge and spread through a series of successive stages: *research*, *development*, and *diffusion* (Figure I.1). It is also linear in a second sense; it assumes that "true" innovations build and improve on one another in an unobstructed march of progress. The heart of this model is what economist Joseph Schumpeter, an early and influential theorist of innovation, called "creative destruction" (Schumpeter, 1939). Put simply, the model's stages reflect the process by which old innovations (e.g., technologies, methods, practices, and organizational strategies) are "disrupted" or destroyed to make room for newer and better ones.

The linear model rose to prominence in World War II, when it became the template for United States government investment in scientific and technological advancement (Godin, 2006). Almost overnight, the federal budget for such research ballooned from $48 to $500 million, as innovation in weapons and defense systems became a matter of national security (Kleinman, 1995). As the war ended, this massive infrastructure for military, industrial, and academic research did not disappear. It just pivoted from producing missiles and bombs to inventing innovations that could address social problems and enhance creature comforts in postwar life. In this process, the linear model expanded its reach from federal science and technology programs to all facets of domestic life, from architecture and urban planning (Light, 2003; Martin, 2003) to the fine arts (Turner, 2013) and education (Urban, 2010). The model's three stages work as follows:

Figure I.1 The linear model of innovation.

RESEARCH	DEVELOPMENT	DIFFUSION
BASIC APPLIED	NEW PRODUCT NEW METHOD NEW MARKET NEW SOURCE OF MATERIALS NEW ORGANIZATION	IMPLEMENTATION SCALING DISRUPTION

- *Research* takes two forms: basic and applied. *Basic* research refers to general study and experimentation that builds knowledge about a subject but is not focused on solving a particular problem. However, if emergent findings suggest potential uses in other contexts, then *applied* research can be conducted to explore how those insights might address issues or inefficiencies elsewhere (Bush, 1945). For example, ARPANET, the precursor to our Internet, began in the 1960s as federally funded basic research on networked computing. It then became the basis for applied research into how the military—and eventually, businesses and individuals—could use this technology.
- *Development* involves translating applied research into an innovation that can be tested and refined. Schumpeter (1939) delineates five categories these innovations tend to fall into: (1) a new product or combination of goods; (2) a new method of creating a product or outcome; (3) a new market that expands the reach of a product or service; (4) a new source of materials for creating or sharing a product; and (5) a new organizational strategy that makes a product or practice more efficient or effective. For instance, the development of smartphones involved a new combination of goods. Applied research related to the Internet, cellular technologies, touch-screen capabilities, and global positioning services (GPS) was merged and developed into a new prototype for mobile communication.
- The *diffusion* stage is where an innovation is implemented into practice and given an opportunity to spread. Ideally, it will be able to disrupt previous ways of doing things. Innovators hope it will become the new standard and its usage can be scaled up (Utterback, 1974). If it fails to do so, according to the model, it likely did not build or improve on past innovations enough to trigger true "disruption." For example, as smartphones transformed from luxury items to widely-used devices, the traditional cellphone and personal digital assistant (PDA) industries were disrupted. When impacted companies tried to adapt and release smartphones of their own, they were quickly dismissed as cheap imitations; they were not sufficiently "innovative" to take attention back from their more disruptive competitors.

It is difficult to overstate the influence the linear model has had in shaping contemporary understandings of innovation. The model remains the foundation for a range of bestselling books, including Clayton Christensen's widely read *The Innovator's Dilemma* (1997) and *The Innovator's Solution* (Christensen & Raynor, 2003), which describe how success and failure are dependent on one's willingness to advance or adapt to "disruptive innovation." The language of "creative destruction" also permeates United States entrepreneurial culture, as industry executives and start-up firms compete to be the next disruptive force in their targeted industry—be it communication, transportation, artificial intelligence, or even space exploration (Taplin, 2017).

This imperative to disrupt has not spared education. The term circulates in dozens of books, including Christensen's own *Disrupting Class* (Christensen et al., 2008), which applies the lessons of disruptive innovation to schools. It is also invoked in sales pitches, press releases, and professional magazines touting the latest technologies, instructional methods, and organizational strategies for classrooms. Even when it is not referenced directly, the logic of the linear model creeps into everyday discussions of teaching and learning. It is at work whenever a change in policy or practice is rationalized on the grounds that it is "the future" or that it will prepare students for forms of employment or living that don't yet exist. The linear model projects visions of an imminent and inevitable future as a justification for disrupting the present.

As commonplace as it is, the linear model has significant shortcomings. It has been critiqued and challenged by historians and economists alike (Edgerton, 1999; Freeman, 1982; Gordon, 2016). For our purposes, three limitations are especially important.

1. *The linear model evaluates the quality or effectiveness of an innovation only in hindsight.* According to the model, an innovation is only truly innovative if it triggers creative disruption—which can never be known in advance. A demand for prescience puts individuals and organizations in the precarious position of constantly placing bets and expending resources on new practices, devices, and strategies on the off chance that they are the next disruptive force in education. By forcing schools to perpetually absorb these risks and costs, the logic of the model skews in favor of those who market or sell educational innovations, not those who implement them.

2. *The linear model is context-agnostic; it does not account for how innovations might have different impacts across locations and communities.* Historians have long shown that linear narratives of progress overlook the local contingencies that shape how innovations are put to use. The invention of telephones and electric lights, for example, did not lead to instantaneous shifts in communication or social life. Rather, these devices were introduced to different communities at different times. In the process, people developed different localized meanings around and practices with them (Marvin, 1983). Put another way, innovations are never implemented in a vacuum. They are layered alongside

already existing innovations into contexts with unique histories and material circumstances. The linear model papers over these dynamics by presenting innovation as flowing through a simplistic succession of stages, irrespective of context.

3. *The linear model locates the origins of innovation outside of the sites where it is applied.* Because it begins with basic research and then extends these insights to particular fields, the linear model positions innovation as an exogenous force. An innovation trickles down into practice from an external (often elite) site of research and development, such as a university, laboratory, think tank, or commercial firm. In education, a trickle-down approach means that much of what traffics as "innovation" does not emerge in response to the situated problems or needs of teachers and students. Instead, what is deemed innovative is an experimental application of someone else's research and development agenda. In the logic of the linear model, schools and classrooms are little more than a testing ground for innovations "from above." Of course, there are times when schools can benefit from this relationship. They might be happy to receive funds or resources from companies, foundations, and philanthropists invested in scaling certain products or practices. But even then, teachers and students are placed at the mercy of innovations they had no part in creating.

Innovation From Below

As I have suggested, this book takes a different starting point for thinking about innovation—an orientation I call *innovation from below.* Where the linear model frames innovation as a spontaneous upshot of creative destruction and assumes that inevitable outcomes will follow its implementation, I argue innovation must be understood in context, as a situated phenomenon, from the ground up. Rather than trying to anticipate the next disruptive force in education, this type of innovation attends to the historical and material circumstances that allow certain ideas, devices, and practices to become available and desirable as "innovations" in schools. It then explores the downstream impacts as they are layered into the everyday life of classrooms. In this way, innovation from below draws from and builds on existing literatures that, similarly, attend to their subject matter "from below" (e.g. Chakrabarty, 1998; Della Porta, 2006).

Innovation from below also shares affinity with similar work in the field of Science and Technology Studies (STS) (Jasanof et al., 1995). "Science from below" (Harding, 2008) has long shown how innovations that appear stable (like scientific discoveries) or inevitable (like technological advancements) actually emerge from precarious processes that are heavily influenced by human decision-making and sociocultural forces (Latour, 1987;

Shapin & Schaffer, 1985). Put another way: from design to implementation, every part of an innovation's development is born of and shot through with politics. As such, we can't really understand how innovations work without attending to the sociopolitical contexts they were formed in and the implications of their uses. Innovation from below is a frame for centering these dynamics by looking at the *interests* and *imperatives* that underwrite innovations and efforts to disrupt teaching and learning.

Interests. Innovation is driven by interests. When someone refers to a new device or strategy as an "innovation," they usually mean that it is innovative *for something*. To them, it advances some larger goal or purpose in education. These purposes are never neutral; they come embedded with the values and priorities of those who fund, greenlight, and produce the innovations to which they are attached. Behind every new device or technique is a series of human choices about what problems should be solved (and how), which resources should be expended (or withheld), and what risks are allowable (and for whom). Importantly, the interests that drive such decisions in the making of an innovation are often at odds with the aims of those who implement and use them. A VR headset manufacturer may be interested in its product's educational potential, but only to the extent that it serves its larger interest in selling lots of VR headsets. The design and development choices that the company makes to advance its financial interest, then, can obstruct or undermine the pedagogical interests of educators who deploy its devices in classrooms. One of the more perverse tricks of the linear model is that it encourages educators not just to adopt innovations that might threaten their interests and values as teachers, but to celebrate such compromises as part of the inevitable march of "progress."

Innovation from below means making the contradictory interests involved in the design and use of innovations visible. When competing interests are papered over by triumphalist tales of "progress," it is easy for certain agendas to overtake others in schools. Historically, such clashes have favored the interests of whiter and wealthier stakeholders. This is not necessarily due to some grand conspiracy, or even the malicious intentions of individuals. Rather, it is because "innovation" as a social phenomenon reflects the biases and injustices of society writ large. Indeed, it is the absence of ill intent behind an innovation's uneven impacts that makes it especially crucial to examine its underlying interests in context. In taking this approach, innovation from below is aligned with research that traces the genealogies of educational practices to understand how the assumptions they inherit (or shed) from the past continue to inflect the present. Flores and García (2017), for example, have shown how the political agenda for community control and racial equity that gave rise to the United States bilingual education movement was excised as this innovation was institutionalized in the post–Civil Rights era—a legacy that endures in contemporary policies and reform efforts. Others, likewise, have demonstrated how popular teaching innovations, from Deweyan learning theories to project-based methods, come freighted with historical assumptions about race, class, and ability that are not easily reconciled with principles that drive their usage today (Fallace, 2015; Johnson, 2000; Schneider, 2014). These perspectives highlight how attending to the underlying interests of innovations is necessary if they are truly to be mobilized to provide a just and equitable education for all.

Imperatives. Innovation is not an additive process. When a device or technique is introduced to a learning environment, what results is not the old environment plus the new innovation, but an entirely new environment. With every such transformation, educators and students must adapt to the norms and practices this new environment demands. We can call these norms and practices *imperatives*. Sometimes changes in the environment are minor, and the imperatives that follow are hardly noticeable. Replacing an old textbook with an updated version, for example, does not fundamentally reshape how teaching and learning proceed. However, a more "disruptive" innovation can manifest imperatives that completely reconfigure activities in and expectations of the classroom. Introducing asynchronous instruction or a new learning management system dramatically reshapes what teaching, assessment, communication, and learning mean and look like. Imperatives, then, play an important role in conditioning what can be said, done, taught, and learned when an innovation is implemented in schools.

This is another way of saying that imperatives are closely tied to power. When people think about power, they usually associate it with force, such as using punishments or fear to bring about particular outcomes. But power can also take less overt (but no less controlling) forms. Social theorist Michel Foucault (1977) called one such form "discipline." Discipline is a type of power that instills ways of thinking and behaving using norms, beliefs, habits, practices, and social pressures (i.e., imperatives) rather than direct force. As people internalize these nudges, they are shaped into particular kinds of people, or what Foucault calls "disciplined subjects." Disciplining the self can be seen in research that shows how schools have historically disciplined students into adopting particular values and dispositions. They are subtly encouraged to follow rules, be punctual, keep quiet, exercise restraint, cooperate with others, and respect authority (Durkheim [1925] 1961; Vallance, 1986). Perhaps not coincidentally, this "hidden curriculum" (Jackson, 1968) of schooling has tended to serve the interests of mostly White, mostly male, mostly wealthy elites who need to frequently replenish their supply of docile workers and happen to have an outsized influence over education policy and reform (Anyon, 1980; Bowles & Gintis, 1976). By foregrounding imperatives, innovation from below explores the ways innovations are not simply introduced into classrooms, but actively discipline educators and students into particular relations with one another and the wider social world.

In doing so, the idea opens space for us to collectively reflect on how these relations might support or undermine the aims of equitable education.

Infrastructures of Innovation

As the example of elites needing workers demonstrates, interests and imperatives are embedded, deliberately or unintentionally, in any innovation. Throughout this book, I show how they actively reshape the ways teaching and learning unfold in contexts where they are introduced. In this way, we can think of innovations as *infrastructural*: The interests and imperatives behind an innovation create infrastructures that condition what happens in schools and classrooms. "Infrastructure" refers to the physical and organizational systems that support particular kinds of practices. Roadways, plumbing networks, and electrical grids are all common infrastructures that people rely on for a variety of work and leisure activities. Anthropologist Susan Leigh Star (1999) suggests that infrastructures often operate so effectively that they fade into the background, becoming invisible to many. When someone turns on a faucet to shower or cook, they probably aren't thinking about the complex infrastructures involved in extracting, decontaminating, and delivering water to them. But when these systems malfunction, Star notes, it becomes easier to see the profound and uneven impacts that infrastructures have on those who rely on them. As I write this, the city of Flint, Michigan, has gone six years without clean water. In an unjust society, being able to take infrastructures for granted is a luxury.

Given the role infrastructures play in supporting everyday practices, a growing research base is now exploring the wider social implications of these infrastructural systems (Edwards et al., 2009). While some of this research retains a focus on traditional, physical infrastructures such as roadways and energy systems, scholars increasingly extend this work to examine forms of infrastructure in other domains (Anand et al., 2020; Bowker & Star, 1999; Mattern, 2014). In education, researchers have explored the infrastructures underpinning daily learning practices in schools. Educational infrastructures guide the ways we organize information in content-area learning (Jurow et al., 2019) and the forms of data we use to drive instructional decision-making (Anagnostopoulos et al., 2013). Penuel (2019, p. 663) helpfully outlines a range of different infrastructures used to support instructional practice in schools:

- Standards for student learning
- Curriculum materials
- Student assessments
- Teacher professional development
- Instructional techniques and routines (e.g., for promoting productive talk in classrooms)

- Building and district level policies (e.g., regarding the posting of standards, submission of lesson plans that follow a particular format)
- School schedules that allocate instructional time for different subjects
- Roles and positions focused on instructional support (e.g., coaches)
- Organizational routines, such as grade-level meetings, in which instruction is a focus
- Personal evaluation systems, including forms of evidence that contribute to assessment of a teacher's performance

Of course, there are other infrastructures we could add to this list that also support modern teaching and learning. Schools routinely use digital technologies to organize and deliver content, and control the structure and arrangement of classroom spaces, for example. What is valuable about Penuel's framing is not its exhaustive accounting of all educational infrastructures, but that it helps us to think infrastructurally about education. The observable teaching and learning that happens in classrooms involves a complex coordination of often-hidden supports. Making these infrastructural supports visible expands our resources for identifying and leveraging opportunities to help all students to flourish.

Thinking infrastructurally also helps us understand the breakdowns and malfunctions that surface as innovations are integrated into practice. Infrastructure is not a fixed category, but a relational one: a plumbing system is infrastructure to a thirsty resident turning on their faucet, but a site of practice to a city planner or engineer. To these workers, infrastructure is dependent on other forms of infrastructure. Like a Matryoshka nesting doll, innovation is infrastructure all the way down. This means that the infrastructures created at one scale can constrain, contradict, or undermine activities at another. Anagnostopoulos and colleagues (2013) illustrate this using the innovation of "data-driven" education. For policymakers, data is an infrastructure for decision-making. But the need for this data requires states and districts to build supplemental infrastructures to collect testing and accountability measures. In turn, these measures require schools and teachers to build additional infrastructures, such as curricula, instructional practices, and assessments to align classrooms with these demands. Even though each of these scales is participating in "data-driven" education, the term means very different things to the people involved. Each must work to navigate the infrastructures imposed on them, some of which may be incompatible with their own aims and values as educators.

What this perspective makes clear is that implementation of an innovation is not a simple, singular, or straightforward process. It is an unruly convergence of competing infrastructures that is contingent on many factors. Innovations are always implemented *somewhere*—in an actual place, with actual people, and conditioned by actual historical and material circumstances. These differences shape every step of the implementation process up to and including the outcomes that result. In papering over these dynamics, the linear model presents innovation as distinct from its social context. The danger of isolating innovation is not just that it leads to wasted time, money, and energy being dumped into trendy innovations that fail in practice. The problem is that imagining innovation as separate from reality also hides explanations or accountability for those failures behind the cloak of "progress." At times, progress can even be used to blame educators and students for innovation's shortcomings. After all, if innovation is a natural linear process, then any issues that arise must stem from those doing the implementing, not the innovations themselves. It is for this reason that innovation from below works to study innovation in use and in context. This means attending to the infrastructures of innovation and the interests and imperatives that shape them. Only then might we understand their downstream implications for educational equity as they are integrated into actual schools and classrooms.

In the chapters that follow, we will use this approach to examine three different types of infrastructures at work in the Innovation School—and as I will suggest, in *any* school striving to be innovative. These include: *imaginative infrastructures*, or the competing ideas people associate with "innovation;" *pedagogical infrastructures,* or the interoperating supports for teaching and learning that underwrite innovative classroom practices; and *technological infrastructures,* or the design decisions behind innovative technologies that manifest distant interests into local school contexts.

What I hope will be clear by the conclusion is that *innovation from below* is not only an analytical frame, but also an agenda for doing educational innovation differently. One reason why the linear model is so pervasive in schools is because it is a fairly realistic depiction of how most educators encounter innovations. Every so often, we get word of new devices, practices, teaching strategies, and curricular add-ons. We are told these are "best practices" or "the future of learning" and that what we had been using is now outdated and obsolete. Because most of us are disconnected from the precarious processes that have gone into making these innovations—full of failed prototypes and paths-not-taken—the whole cycle feels intuitive and inevitable.

In taking an alternate orientation—innovation from below—this book demonstrates that a naturalized linear approach is not the most helpful way to think about innovation. Attending to infrastructure is an effective way to challenge more conventional ideas about innovation by attuning educators not only to the shortcomings of the linear model, but also to the possibilities that alternate infrastructures—driven by equity and student flourishing—might hold for our classrooms. One goal of this book, then, is that it can help to situate innovation as something that emerges from the lived experiences, challenges, and opportunities of actual schools. We need to stop rooting our notion of innovation in someone else's vision of what "21st century learning" or the "future of education" ought to look like, and instead, ground it in what will best serve *today's* students in *today's* classrooms. In taking this stance, I draw inspiration from and build upon the rich traditions of practitioner inquiry and teacher research that have long recognized classrooms as rich sites for producing knowledge and innovating from below (Cochran-Smith & Lytle, 2009; Ghiso et al., 2013).

OUTLINE OF THE BOOK

There are four main arguments that are reinforced in different ways throughout the rest of this book. They are, in short:

- "Innovation," as it is commonly used in education, tends to advance national-economic and corporate interests over those of schools and communities. This orientation works against alternate values like autonomy, democracy, and the public good.
- The imperative toward "disruption" is fundamentally incompatible with efforts to build sustainable infrastructures for equitable teaching and learning.
- The impacts of innovations fall unevenly on stakeholders. Those who are insulated from the risks and costs of "disruption" are given advantage; those who are not are individually blamed for systemic shortcomings.
- Relocating innovation in the lived dynamics of schools can mobilize alternate infrastructures, driven by interests and imperatives that serve the aims and values of equity and human flourishing.

Each chapter focuses on forms of infrastructure that conditioned the meaning, uses, and impacts of innovation in the Innovation School.

Chapter 1, *Imaginative Infrastructures*, explores how different stakeholders hold competing ideas about what constitutes innovation in schools. It suggests that these "imaginative infrastructures" guide how schools and classrooms are designed. By following how the Innovation School's model was shaped, implemented, and adapted over time, the chapter also demonstrates how competing imaginaries produced conflicting imperatives. These imperatives sometimes worked against the efforts of students, who had their own ideas about what was most innovative about the school.

Chapter 2, *Pedagogical Infrastructures*, examines how different instructional innovations introduced in the Innovation School interoperated with one another. Contrary to the linear model, it demonstrates that innovations are not just disruptive shocks. Rather, innovations actively remake the working infrastructures of teaching and learning on which many students and teachers depend. The chapter then follows how different types of school infrastructure were reconfigured as teachers turned a humanities classroom into an asynchronous makerspace. This renovation opened exciting possibilities for students poised to take advantage of them, but also created new and unanticipated challenges for others—raising questions about how such diverse outcomes can be reconciled in innovative classrooms.

Chapter 3, *Technological Infrastructures,* considers the interests and imperatives that are embedded in classroom technologies. It first explores how devices that are intended to support autonomous or asynchronous learning can introduce forms of surveillance and predictive analytics that undermine these goals in practice. It also illustrates how infrastructures of digital platforms (e.g., hardware, interfaces, algorithms, code), at times thwarted students' creative and composing practices in subtle ways that were only visible to teachers or researchers later. It argues that attending to these hidden dynamics not only has implications for how educators think about and use technologies in the classroom, but also offers possibilities for foregrounding digital infrastructures as a site of instruction and inquiry for students.

Chapter 4, *Innovating from Below,* builds on the preceding chapters. In this chapter I argue that while many of the innovations implemented "from above" created infrastructural tensions in the classroom, some of the practices at the margins of the school show how an alternate orientation to innovation is possible. It develops this innovation-from-below perspective though a case study of an innovation that took shape over multiple years— the Literacy Lab. What began as a common workspace stocked with books and resources for students gradually evolved to address a variety of other needs that emerged from the school's model. This chapter demonstrates how even ostensibly mundane resources, when targeted to the needs and desires of students and teachers, can have even more profound impacts on learning than devices and strategies that are passed down from above as "innovative."

In concluding, the book steps back to take a wider view of its overarching theme: how educational innovations centered on disruption reproduce inequality by failing to build durable infrastructures that support all students. It suggests that the alternative—innovation from below—offers a powerful reorientation from disruptive intervention toward an ethic of repair. That is, it attunes us to the underlying infrastructures on which equitable, just, and liberatory teaching and learning depend. "Repair," in this sense, does not mean restoring an object to a prior condition, but transforming the conditions in which that object operates. From this perspective, it becomes possible to see public schools—and their yet unfulfilled promise of equitable education for all—as one of the most ambitious innovations we've ever attempted. Even more, a reparative orientation directs our attention to the infrastructures we need to defend, enrich, and sustain the integrity of this bold innovation. In this way, it is repair, not disruption, that offers the clearest path for public education to live up to its most revolutionary possibilities.

CHAPTER 1

Imaginative Infrastructures

A colorless conference room deep in the School District of Philadelphia's central office isn't the most obvious place to start exploring educational innovation. But for the Innovation School's founding teachers, that's where the idea of innovation went from being an abstract aspiration to a complicated reality. Most were experienced educators with long histories in the district. They had developed reputations for carving out space in conventional classrooms for inventive instruction. These reputations led Ben, the school's founding principal, to recruit them in the spring of 2014 to be part of a new initiative to, in his words, "put students at the center of schooling." His proposition sounded inspiring to the teachers. But now it was summer, 2 months before the Innovation School was to open, and details were still hazy about how this ambitious goal would be realized. The desire for innovation had to be translated into concrete daily learning practices. This was the task that brought the teachers and Ben together for a summer planning session in a secluded corner of the central office.

Ben opened the first meeting with a welcome message, outlining his vision for the school. He spoke of the inequities plaguing the education system and of the recent cuts to the district's spending. He told them he wanted the Innovation School to chart a new path for teaching and learning in Philadelphia and beyond. Teachers nodded in affirmation as he described students taking ownership of their education, working independently on real-world problems in the school's makerspaces and core classes. Over the rest of the morning, teachers brainstormed the policies and practices needed to support such innovations. The conversations were electric and alive with possibility. It was when the group returned from lunch that obstacles began to appear. First, a representative from the organization that provided financial support to open the Innovation School gave a short presentation about the competency-based standards the teachers would be expected to implement. Then a district official visited to explain how the central office would convert these competencies into numerical scores for accountability purposes. Over the week, more information sessions followed. They were told about student Chromebooks, design thinking, and project-based learning. It was becoming clear that building the school's model would involve more than just implementing innovative ideas. Teachers were caught in the middle, coordinating different stakeholders' competing understandings of what exactly "innovation" was.

This chapter explores what happens when different ideas about innovation are layered together in classrooms. It follows the process by which the Innovation School's model was shaped and reshaped in response to the pressures and priorities of the district, teachers, and students. I show how "innovation imaginaries"—the ways different stakeholders envisioned innovative education—operated as a form of classroom infrastructure that powerfully oriented teaching and learning toward particular imperatives. Promising learning opportunities can open up in moments when stakeholders' imaginaries are aligned. However, when incongruities surface, frictions and frustrations for teachers and students can result (cf. Nichols & Coleman, 2021; Stornaiuolo & Nichols, 2018; 2020). Attending to imaginative infrastructures, I argue, delivers valuable insights into how "innovation" is put to work in schools, and whose understandings are truly prioritized in the process.

INNOVATION IMAGINARIES

When I teach or lead workshops about educational innovation, I often start by sharing a 19th-century French postcard that envisioned what a school might look like in the year 2000 (Figure 1.1). In the image, a teacher feeds books into a crank-operated machine that converts the texts into information, transmitted into the wired headsets of docile students who obediently absorb the curriculum. What I like about this print is that it highlights how educational innovation is closely tied to the imagination—and specifically, to the ways we imagine the future. While the linear model asserts that innovations "disrupt" the present and usher in new ways of being, this picture is striking not because of what the innovation (i.e., the Book Conversion Machine) disrupts, but what it leaves intact. My students are quick to point out the assumptions this imagined future preserves from the past. Teachers are primarily content-deliverers, and students simply absorb information. Learning remains primarily a transmission of book knowledge. We might go further still and note that it was easier for the artist to imagine a new book-to-audio conversion technology than a classroom with nonwhite people, women, or equal learning conditions (one student must operate the crank so the others can learn). From this perspective, innovation is a force less of disruption than of continuity. It threatens to be a conduit for advancing conservative present-day interests and assumptions by materializing certain imagined futures over others.

The way we imagine innovation in education is never neutral. To envision an innovative school is to make a statement about what kinds of practices, devices, and dispositions are desirable. In the process, the vision also

Figure 1.1. 19th-century French print representing the future of schooling

Source. Image from unproduced postcard series by Jean-Marc Côté and other artists, c. 1900. Wikimedia Commons

defines the practices that ought to be excluded from classrooms. The imagination is a powerful infrastructure for conditioning what the social world of school looks, sounds, and feels like. It establishes imperatives for classrooms that shape what is said, done, taught, and learned in them. The philosopher Charles Taylor (2003) uses the term "social imaginary" to describe the world-making power of the imagination. For Taylor, a social imaginary is a tacit understanding that people have about how the world ought to work in the future. These understandings give rise to norms and practices (i.e., "imperatives") that allow those who share them to find a common sense of purpose and legitimacy as they work to align the world of the present with the aspirational future they imagine (Taylor, 2007, p. 199). We can see the pull of social imaginaries in that first meeting of the Innovation School faculty in the district's central office.

As Ben outlined his vision for the school, he didn't appeal to a specific or technical definition of innovation. Rather, he relied on an intuitive idea of what an innovative classroom is. Teachers were able to nod along affirmingly because they could recognize features in his description that resonated with their own implicit understandings of educational innovation. I call such shared understandings *innovation imaginaries.* When I invited you to picture an "innovative" classroom at the start of this book, I was asking you to articulate your own innovation imaginary: *your* tacit understanding of what innovation means and looks like in school. As I noted, it's possible that your imaginary might align with or diverge from a colleague's or senior administrator's. This is why the plural form of "imaginaries" is significant; to Taylor, heterogenous understandings of innovation never exist in isolation. Competing imaginaries often overlap or bump up against one another, particularly in educational spaces.

Anthropologist Arjun Appadurai (1990) suggests we might think of imaginaries as flows circulating within and between social worlds. Sometimes these flows coexist harmoniously with one another. At other times they jockey for position or create frictions. For instance, when the representative from the funding organization addressed the Innovation School's teachers, she emphasized competency-based standards—something central to the innovation imaginary of her employer but not necessarily to that of the teachers. However, because competency-based standards did not actively conflict with the teachers' imaginary, these competing flows were able to coexist more readily than some of the other "innovative" expectations laid out that week. Adopting an orientation of *innovation from below* means not taking intuitive ideas about innovation for granted. Rather, it encourages us to make imaginative infrastructures visible. Doing so can help us better understand the interests and imperatives that drive different conceptions of innovation and the uneven impacts that result when competing imaginaries intermingle and collide.

MAPPING THE IMAGINARY

Visualizing an innovation imaginary first requires us to delineate how "innovation" is associated in a given context with specific goals and purposes. These goals are not limited to teachers and students, they are also held by stakeholders with a role in shaping the learning environment, like senior administrators and funders. By analyzing fieldnotes, interviews, and recordings of district- and school-level professional development over 3 years, we can define five categories of goals or purposes in the Innovation School: *content-area learning, technoscience, autonomy, entrepreneurship,* and *social justice.* Table 1.1 offers a description of each, along with examples.

These categories aren't universal, nor do they encapsulate all possible categories that could be present in a school. They are simply the categories most referenced and emphasized over the Innovation School's first 3 years. Mapping an innovation imaginary in another context could result in a very different set of categories (see online appendix at www.tcpress.com /building-the-innovation-school-9780807766781 for a walkthrough of how you can map the innovation imaginary of your own site of practice). While some of these categories are fairly distinct, others can blur together. "Social justice," for instance, often emphasizes forms of collective action that may not sit as easily with certain kinds of individualized "autonomy." "Content-area learning," by contrast, can play nicely with makerspaces and other

Table 1.1: Categories of innovation in the Innovation School

Category	Description	Example
Content-area learning	Innovation intended to support the depth or breadth of students' engagements with disciplinary learning	Competency-based standards; project-based learning
Technoscience	Innovation geared toward (1) increasing accessibility of or contact with technologies; or (2) extending science/STEM learning across disciplines	One-to-one devices; interdisciplinary makerspaces
Autonomy	Innovation that decenters formal/direct instruction and gives students greater choice and flexibility in what, when, and how they learn.	Asynchronous learning, adaptive technologies
Entrepreneurship	Innovation that encourages the design and creation of products, often (but not always) in response to real-world problems	Design thinking; 20% Time / Genius Hour
Social justice	Innovation in teaching and learning that emphasizes (1) nondominant or marginalized perspectives, (2) critical engagement with issues of inequity, and/or (3) forms of civic action and activism in- or outside of school.	Culturally relevant pedagogy; action-civics projects

forms of "technoscience" that support rich scientific inquiry (Nichols & Lui, 2019; Salisbury & Nichols, 2020). For this reason, it is helpful to think about these categories not as fixed goals, but as diverse imperatives whose relations to one another help define the shape an innovation imaginary takes.

From here, we can begin to map the relations of these categories. As I have already suggested, the innovation that Ben and the teachers had in mind was driven by different priorities than that of the funding organization. The organization—and by extension, the district—expected competency-based standards and content-area learning to be the central features of an innovative education. The district emphasized STEM-based learning and 1:1 technologies in its vision. These points were reflected in the press release that announced the Innovation School's opening. This is not to suggest the district was opposed to the other categories, only that they did not hold the same weight. Ben and the teachers, however, saw innovation differently.

Figure 1.2. Mapping innovation imaginaries of the district (L) and the Innovation School (R)

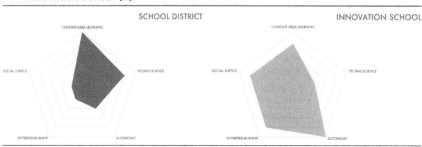

Technology and STEM learning were secondary to autonomy, entrepreneurship, and social justice education. While they shared the district's interest in content-area learning, their emphasis was more widely distributed to the other categories. We can represent these similarities and differences by estimating the weight different stakeholders accorded to each category (on a scale from one to five) and plotting them on a radar chart (Figure 1.2). Doing so allows us to begin seeing how the relations between these categories gives the resulting innovation imaginary a particular shape. Of course, this isn't an exact science, and it does oversimplify certain small variations that existed among district officials and teachers. However, mapping the broad patterns in stakeholders' conceptions of innovation helps spotlight the competing ways the idea was mobilized.

COMPETING IMAGINARIES, CONFLICTING IMPERATIVES

When we overlay the innovation imaginaries of the district and school, we begin to get a sense of the different pressures at work when "innovation" is implemented into practice (Figure 1.3). There is a significant area of overlap between the two imaginaries, which is what allowed district officials and teachers to even discuss ideas about innovation together. However, the asymmetries are significant, and reflect diverging imperatives about the norms and practices to be embedded into classrooms under the name of innovation.

Because the school operated under the purview of the district, teachers could not simply implement their own innovation imaginary; they had to do so while accommodating the demands and expectations passed down from above. The result was a combination of "innovative" impulses that were sometimes puzzling. For instance, while the funder and district had provided money to equip the school with a Media Makerspace (in line with their emphasis on technoscience), the teachers saw the value of makerspaces

Figure 1.3. Overlay of district and school innovation imaginaries

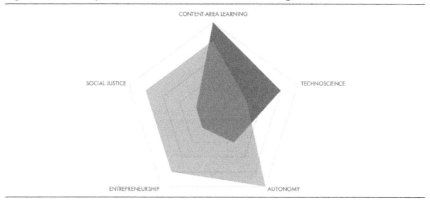

as opportunities for self-directed learning and creative production (in line with their emphases on autonomy and entrepreneurship). As such, the finished makerspace looked less like a conventional, technology-rich makerspace and more like a large open classroom with space for students to move about freely as they created projects (see Figure 1.4).

Frictions like these became more pronounced once the school officially opened. Suddenly, all of the abstract theorizing about innovation that had taken place among district officials and teachers throughout the summer was put to the test. Students—with their own imaginaries of what an innovative school ought to look, sound, and feel like—entered the picture. Just before the school year began, incoming students attended an open house to meet their teachers and tour the facility. Many were quick to express how different the school was from the sort of "innovative" environment they had pictured. Some were surprised by the building, which was actually the second floor of an elementary school that had been shuttered a year prior during a round of district budget cuts. Others had enrolled in the school based on the district's promises that it would emphasize technology-driven learning. They were caught off guard by the lack of high-tech equipment throughout the school. One student commented, "It isn't any different from my old school."

These incongruities persisted through the first weeks of the school year. Almost immediately, many students began asking when they would receive the one-to-one computers that had been promised to them upon enrollment. The teachers, however, wanted to emphasize that the school's focus was not just on tools and technology, but on autonomous learning. To make this clear, they devised a week-long, school-wide activity that would introduce students to the competency-based learning that would be central to the core classes and makerspaces. Students were issued a "passport" that listed clusters of tasks and activities related to the school learning model

Figure 1.4. Media Makerspace setup for the first week of school.

and responsible technology usage. The clusters could be completed independently or collaboratively, and in whatever order students wished. As they finished activities, students travelled to different parts of the school to have teachers stamp their passports before proceeding to their next set of activities. Once their passports were completed, they could submit them to Ben and receive their school-issued Chromebooks.

The Passport Activity elicited mixed responses from students. Some felt they were victims of an innovation bait-and-switch: they had enrolled in the school because they believed it would be similar to the selective technology-rich schools in the area. Instead of being ushered into a shiny environment full of devices, they were asked to jump through hoops to earn competencies and demonstrate autonomy before they could even use a computer. When members of our research team asked students if the school was what they expected, several students expressed confusion about the school model. One student summed up this sentiment, saying, "I thought it was going to be better than other high schools. Then I got here and I realized it's the same . . . the same drama, the same teachers. We just get competencies instead of report cards." This disconnect was enough of a frustration that nine students (nearly a tenth of its founding cohort) withdrew from the school in its first weeks. This was, understandably, disappointing for the teachers.

They gathered every day after school in the Media Makerspace to debrief the day's successes and challenges. These conversations were often tearful, full of frustration as to why their efforts to create an innovative learning environment that gave students choice and flexibility would be met with such resistance.

But there were also encouraging breakthroughs. In completing the passport activity, some students recognized the educational possibilities that asynchronous, competency-based learning could offer. They were excited by the prospect of being able to tailor assignments to their own interests and complete them at their own pace. Even though these were not necessarily the primary reasons students had enrolled in the Innovation School, the potential was promising enough that some stretched their imaginaries to better fit the model being offered by the school. One such student, Tyrell, theorized that the reason some of his classmates had withdrawn from the school was because they struggled to adapt their imagination: "It's so new and different, they just couldn't wrap their heads around it. . . . It was so innovative [that] I don't think they understood it enough to want to stay and figure it out." In other words, those students who could align their imaginaries to that of the school were able to recognize the innovation at work. For those who wanted a more familiar form of innovation, even the most "innovative" features that the district and teachers had put into place read as stale and ordinary.

IMAGINARY ALIGNMENTS: THE MEDIA MAKERSPACE

This disconnect became more pronounced as the school year continued— perhaps most visibly in the school's makerspaces. In core classes, teachers quickly realized that the ideal of asynchronous learning—where students worked through assignments on their own schedule—would require more preparation and resources to implement than were available to them. As a result, the math, science, and humanities classes temporarily pivoted to a synchronous model that retained a focus on inquiry-driven, project-based learning. For much of the first year, the makerspaces were the primary location where the school's unadulterated vision of innovation endured.

In the Media Makerspace, the teacher Sam—a veteran educator who also taught the school's humanities classes—framed the course around "Wicked Problems" (i.e., complex social issues that don't have easy solutions; cf. Rittel & Webber, 1973). He told students that the Media Makerspace was a place where they would have unstructured time to devise and carry out creative projects to address the Wicked Problems that were most meaningful or pressing to them. Sam and the other teachers referred to this pairing of creative production and social problem solving as "social entrepreneurship." This concept, along with the focus on independent, asynchronous learning, braided the school imaginary's emphasis on social justice together with entrepreneurship and autonomy. It was in places like the Media Makerspace where students' imaginaries most directly encountered the imaginaries of the teachers. We can learn about what happens when competing imaginaries flow together in classrooms by looking at the alignments, partial alignments, and misalignments that surfaced in this conflicted space.

Alignment: Crystal's Gentrification Talk Show

Crystal was a gregarious and cheerful 15-year-old who could light up any room that she entered. A talented performer, she was a leader of the school dance team and aspired to be an actor and singer. She was also curious and observant; after hearing the adults in her life talking about "gentrification," she began to investigate the concept. It became the basis for a self-directed research project in Sam's humanities class. In her study, she learned that a local university near the school in her neighborhood had been acquiring property to expand its facilities. Their real estate speculation was, in turn, driving up the cost of living for longtime residents. Initially, she submitted her findings in a research paper. However, after hearing Sam describe how the Media Makerspace could be used, she realized that she could leverage its resources to circulate her ideas more widely. In the process, she could raise awareness about the Wicked Problem of gentrification.

Apart from the short videos she made for friends and followers on social media, Crystal did not have much prior experience with media production. But she wasn't especially concerned about making a technologically advanced or neatly polished presentation. Her main focus was, in her words, "getting ideas out in the world." A fan of talk shows, she decided to adopt this format in her media project. She mounted one of the school's flimsy Flipcams to a tripod and arranged chairs in the makerspace to simulate a talk-show set. She then proceeded to interview classmates about their awareness of gentrification and its impact on their neighborhoods and communities. Periodically, she would pause from these interviews to address the camera directly, sharing facts and figures from her research.

In creating her talk show, we can see how Crystal's use of the Media Makerspace closely aligned to the educational imaginary promoted by the teachers. She demonstrated autonomy in using the unstructured time and space of the classroom to translate her outside interests and research into a meaningful media product. Likewise, her emphasis on social entrepreneurship was about more than technological complexity. Creating products that intervened in matters of social justice accorded with the teachers' priorities. Even the weight given to content-area learning harmonized with the school model; while research was a necessary precursor for creating the project, the power of the video hinged on the urgency with which it conveyed its message of social justice. As Crystal put it, "The paper was more information. The video was more about my opinion. . . . I live in that area; what if it was to happen to me?" Given these alignments, it is not surprising that the teachers quickly recognized Crystal's project as an exemplar of innovative learning that the school design made possible. It was elevated to other students as an aspirational model. Sam even sent the video to the central office, where it was screened at a district meeting of teachers and administrators as a demonstration of the innovative work happening at the school.

Partial Alignment: Devi's Gun Violence Digital Story

However, not all students shared Crystal's experience of finding immediate synergies between their ideas about innovative learning and the school's makerspaces. For most, their alignments with the school model were fragmentary. At times, students' conceptions of innovation matched the school's, allowing them to produce powerful creative work. At other times, partial alignments left students feeling disconnected from the imperatives and norms of the classroom. Devi was one such example. Devi was an enthusiastic storyteller, music lover, and basketball player. But his enthusiasm seemed to dissipate in the Media Makerspace. He had enrolled in the school because he thought it was going to have the same technologies as the selective science magnet schools in the district. However, on arrival, he found the technology to be similar to his old school. Like many students, he spent time in the Media Makerspace sitting at a table with earbuds in, listening to music or watching YouTube videos, then pretending to be busy whenever the teacher walked by to check on his progress.

When Sam asked him what Wicked Problem he was interested in, Devi said gun violence. Later, he confessed to research team members that he'd only picked the topic because it was the example Sam used when introducing the project, and that he wasn't feeling motivated to get started on the assignment. His interest was piqued, however, as he watched his classmates making films and podcasts and infographics related to their Wicked Problems. Due to the short supply of media technologies in the makerspace, the research team had borrowed cameras, boom mics, and lighting equipment from the university and made them available to the students. Devi was pressed into service to help direct a friend's video, which gave him an opportunity to experiment with the high-tech devices he'd imagined would be part of the school environment. Almost immediately, he began to see possibilities for how he could use these media technologies in his own project. He began talking with members of the research team about his own story of growing up in Liberia, making connections between gun violence there and in his current city. He became animated, sketching an outline for a digital story that knitted together video footage, spoken word poetry, and images of Liberia and Philadelphia.

Devi's experience is an example of a partial alignment between a student and teachers' innovation imaginary. In the end, Devi's project involved many of the imperatives that drove the school's vision of innovative learning. He worked autonomously and brought his interests and identity to bear on his schoolwork. Devi engaged in a form of social entrepreneurship similar to that celebrated in Crystal's project. However, these categories were not intrinsically the most motivating factors for Devi. It was the presence of technological tools—a category of innovation the teachers were less invested in—that stimulated his interest in the project and allowed other areas of alignment to take shape. In a strange turn, the misalignment between his own educational imaginary and that of the teachers allowed him to work within the school model.

Misalignment: Kalif's Police Brutality Infographic

Importantly, there were also students for whom the misalignments with the school imaginary did not produce moments of harmony. There are many reasons why students or their families might choose to enroll in an "innovative" school. Not all of those reasons are strictly linked to technology, autonomy, or other categories that district leaders or teachers find desirable. For Kalif, the decision to attend the Innovation School wasn't based on innovative features, but simply on mitigating risk. Kalif's neighborhood high school was among those that had been shuttered the year prior, and its former students had been reassigned to other schools in the area. The new school that Kalif would have been assigned to was already overcrowded and understaffed before the closures. His family rightly worried that these conditions, now exacerbated with an influx of new students, would negatively impact his learning. Under these circumstances, the district's advertised "innovation" initiative began to look promising. The schools would be smaller, and they promised to replicate the successes of selective magnet schools in the area. While there was risk involved in attending a new, untested school, Kalif and his family saw a higher ceiling of possibility at the Innovation School than at his neighborhood school.

Given his reasons for enrolling in the school, Kalif was understandably disoriented by some of the innovative imperatives at work in the Media Makerspace. The imperative for autonomy meant there was flexibility in how students managed their time. However, in practice, this resulted in semi-organized chaos. Students oscillated between experiments in media production, hanging out with friends, listening to music or watching videos, and napping. Likewise, the imperatives for social justice and entrepreneurship gave direction to the kinds of projects students were to be creating, but the expectations for what these projects should include and how they would be assessed against the content-area competencies were less clear. It was evident, in other words, that "success" meant and looked different in the makerspace than it did in other classes and schools.

A lack of guidance became frustrating for Kalif as he worked on his Wicked Problem project, an infographic about police brutality. To gather information for the infographic, Sam encouraged Kalif to create a survey that could be distributed to students, teachers, and their networks. Sam sat with him at one of the classroom computers explaining how to create a survey using Google Forms. He then left Kalif to draft questions that could be included on the survey, periodically returning to check in on his progress. Over two class periods, Kalif wrote 15 questions—a mix of yes/no and multiple-choice prompts—to gather data for his infographic. When he proudly showed these to Sam, he was surprised and irritated that Sam suggested revisions before he could proceed. One question, for instance, asked about the causes of police brutality, and Sam pushed him to consider whether the choices given ("power, stupidity, ignorance, or fear") could be more distinct and precise. I sat with Kalif as he revised his questions. He was annoyed and confused. Repeatedly he said that he just wanted to do what he had to do to get a good grade on the assignment. If he was going to be evaluated on the infographic that he produced, he didn't understand why Sam was making him jump through hoops tweaking survey questions.

Kalif's frustration illustrates how misalignments between students' and teachers' imaginaries could lead to competing imperatives in the classroom. In this instance, it was not obvious to Kalif whether he was being assessed on the design of his infographic (which aligned to the aims of social justice and entrepreneurship) or on his ability to produce a reliable survey (which aligned with content-area learning). When Sam offered him feedback on the latter, Kalif understood it to be a distraction from his work on the former. In his case, the makerspace's imperative toward autonomy meant that there was not always explicit explanations or guidance to clarify such contradictions. As a result, Kalif's own desire to navigate the expectations of the classroom and get a good grade became muddled by other pressures in this learning context.

INNOVATION IN THE "MAKING"

Reading these examples with an eye toward innovation imaginaries helps reveal the hidden infrastructures that conditioned teaching and learning in the Media Makerspace over the school's first year. While it would be easy to interpret alignments like Crystal's as "successful" and misalignments (such as Devi's or Kalif's) as "unsuccessful," a focus on imaginaries complicates matters. Indeed, from a standpoint of imaginaries, all three students' responses to the Media Makerspace were perfectly reasonable. Crystal recognized that the flexibility of the class allowed her to extend her interests and research in new directions, meaning that she enthusiastically embraced the model. But Devi and Kalif's motivations were also legitimate. Both had arrived at the school with an imaginary shaped by the district's promotional materials; the classrooms would be technology-rich and offer content-area instruction on par with more selective schools in the area. In the absence of these features, they were understandably cautious about how to learn in the makerspace. It is telling, for instance, that it was only when Devi saw the cameras and boom mics that he began to recognize a resonance between the school imaginary and his own. Only then did he start to engage in the Wicked Problems project. Attention to the imaginative infrastructures of innovation can help us to see these varied outcomes not as the individual successes or shortcomings of students. Rather, they are the result of competing imperatives coming together in the shared space of the classroom.

The trouble is that the linear model of innovation—the orientation most prevalent in schools and public discourse—gets the relationship between learning and innovation backwards. In positioning innovation as passed down from above, it interprets misalignments not as opportunities to explain or reconcile differing perspectives about learning, but as deviations that need to be corrected or disrupted. The linear model is so pervasive that even compassionate, justice-oriented teachers and researchers can default to this logic if they don't have a viable framework to counter it. During the school's first year, the researchers and teachers had not yet articulated a framework for understanding innovation imaginaries. As a result, over the following summer, conversations centered less on interrogating the assumptions of innovation baked into the school model. Instead, they celebrated the handful of students like Crystal who "got it." Although well-meaning, they started devising strategies to help those students who "didn't get it" to adapt. Ben's words to teachers during summer professional planning encapsulated this desire: "Some students need stepping-stones to get to full autonomy. Undoing eight years of acculturation doesn't happen overnight. When we encounter resistance [from students], it's not disrespect—we're disrupting their view of the world."

Summer planning before the second year started to focus on creating these "stepping-stones to autonomy." The first task involved reviving asynchronous learning in the math, science, and humanities classes. The teachers believed that the uneven outcomes in the makerspaces the year before could be the result of the mixed messages they were sending about the value of asynchronous education. They were concerned that some students might be understanding the asynchronous, autonomous learning of the makerspaces as distinct (and, perhaps, less "real") than the more structured learning taking place in content-area classes. This concern was substantiated in year-end interviews, in which many students described the makerspaces as "fun" but didn't necessarily see them as places where "real learning" happened. In one student's words, "We didn't really learn anything or do anything there. We had a good time, but there was always stuff being thrown around and it was always loud." To help students recognize this chaos and energy as integral parts of autonomous learning, the teachers were determined to close the "divide" between the core classes and makerspace by remaking the former in the image of the latter.

We will explore the substance and implications of these shifts over the school's second year in Chapter 2, but some key dynamics are relevant to our discussion of imaginaries. Most importantly, all of the adjustments reflected the school imaginary's prioritization of autonomy over other forms of educational innovation. The teachers restructured the curriculum into "playlists" of readings, viewings, quizzes, and activities that could be completed in whatever order and pace students wished. The classroom space was, likewise, reconfigured to allow for free movement between designated areas for independent or collaborative work. Teachers also developed routines and rituals that would give order to the otherwise unstructured time. For example, when students arrived at a class, they would complete a "Daily Action Plan," which would allow them to identify learning goals from their playlists each day (Figure 1.5). Teachers would also use these to monitor students' progress in a given unit, and would follow up with students in one-on-one conferences.

The clearest illustration of the prioritization of autonomy in the revised school model was also the most controversial. Through conversations with a consultant who specialized in asynchronous learning, Ben determined that the only way to ensure that teachers would have time and energy to establish and maintain asynchronous learning in the classroom would be to take some of the classroom instruction off their plates—at least, in the

Figure 1.5. Daily Action Plan (DAP) created to scaffold autonomous learning.

Name:			
MONDAY **Daily Action Plan** **Date:**	Activities from Unit Guide ☐ ☐ ☐	By the end of the class period, I will...	Doodle Box / Daily Q
End of Class Reflection	How did I do today?  ☺ 😐 ☹	What did you accomplish today? How did you accomplish it? What do I need to do for HW or tomorrow?	

short term. While the teachers would still be responsible for organizing the new unit "playlists," the content-area lessons that comprised them would be delivered through a third-party digital learning platform. This way, teachers could focus their attention on using coaching and feedback to foster students' autonomous learning habits. Ben emphasized that this decision was not ideal, but he worried that asking teachers to establish the norms of asynchronous learning while also creating and delivering lessons would be "trying to do too much too quickly." The teachers, too, were torn. They were committed to the idea of autonomy, but they were not sure it was worth sacrificing the quality of content-area learning in order to cultivate it. On a walk to the train station with Sam just after this plan was introduced, he expressed to me the friction he felt between his experience as a teacher and the larger vision of the school. "I'm going to be a team player for my colleagues," he said, "but I'm not sure about this." In the language we have used throughout this chapter, we can understand the tension Sam described as a misalignment between his own imaginary, shaped by years of experience as a content-area teacher, and the top-down imperative reinforced in the school model.

THE IMPERATIVES OF AUTONOMY

The renewed emphasis on autonomy going into the second year helps illustrate how power is infused with the ways we imagine innovative education. On the surface, this may sound counterintuitive. When we think about how power is exerted in schools, "cultivating student autonomy" probably isn't what jumps to mind. Indeed, for the Innovation School teachers, the focus on autonomy was intended as a *counterpoint* to forms of schooling that rely on top-down impositions of force. When orienting new students to the school, educators often invoked the popular image of a "factory-model" education—in which students are viewed as passive widgets, tracked and sorted through mechanistic and inhumane processes as a contrast to their own orientation toward self-directed learning (for an account of the broad usage, and questionable history, of this "factory" metaphor see Schneider, 2015). But as we have already noted, power is not only manifested through force. It is also a kind of discipline: a means of shaping beliefs, norms, and practices to fit an imagined expectation (Foucault, 1977). From this perspective, valuing autonomy exerts power by establishing imperatives that encourage some ways of being more than others. These imperatives are not necessarily bad, but they are never neutral. And as Sam's uncertainties about the school model demonstrate, they can also have unintended consequences, even for those who ostensibly share their underlying values. For these reasons, it is important to understand the impacts and outcomes that surface as these imperatives are embedded in schools.

Though the imperatives of autonomy were visible the summer before the second year—dramatically reworking the routines, spaces, and instructional practices of classrooms—they were most pronounced when students returned. While some students quickly adapted to the new changes, many were puzzled by the lack of structure. Those who had wished for more technology-rich learning in the first year voiced that watching virtual lectures and completing quizzes wasn't what they had in mind. Those students who had envisioned deep, content-area learning wondered what the point of coming to school was if instruction was online. "It's like the teachers aren't even teaching," one student said, summarizing the consensus of her friends. Students quickly devised clever workarounds to subvert the virtual lessons. They opened multiple windows to consult their notes during quizzes and rebooted the computer before quiz scores were recorded so they could retake them until they passed. Still more students realized that if they skipped these virtual components on the playlist and went right to the more engaging end-of-unit projects, they could still earn enough competencies to pass the unit—even if they never completed the content-area lessons.

It was becoming clear that students were not following Ben's "stepping-stones to autonomy" in the way he and the teachers anticipated. With the district looking over their shoulders for results from its investment in innovative education, they were beginning to feel pressure. In the middle of the fall semester, Ben and the teachers determined the best path forward was to group students by level of autonomy. Those who were successfully navigating the unstructured makerspace-inspired model were termed "semi-autonomous," and would continue through the curriculum as planned. The rest would be placed in "teacher-supported" or "teacher-directed" classes. The former would balance synchronous teacher-led instruction with asynchronous activities; the latter would replicate a more traditional synchronous classroom. Students' placements in these classes were negotiated through conferences with teachers, in which they reviewed their progress and discussed their learning preferences.

In introducing these autonomy-based groupings, teachers stressed that students were not being categorized by their abilities but by the supports they needed to be independent learners. For those students who understood and shared the school's imagined ideal of autonomy, this distinction made sense. In her interview, Crystal—who was naturally assigned to the semi-autonomous class—explained, "A lot of students think they're being categorized, like, 'the semi-autonomous are the smartest and the teacher-directed are the kids who aren't smart.' But it's really just categorizing you on how much you can be independent." However, as Crystal implied, many of the students who were already straining to navigate the norms of the school model regarded these groupings as a form of ability tracking. Despite explicit messaging from teachers that the different classes were not better or worse than one another, assumptions about their hierarchy crept into the school's daily language. Students like Devi and Kalif, who were assigned to the teacher-supported class, often talked about "moving up" to the semi-autonomous class. When those in the semi-autonomous class struggled to keep pace with their assignments, they were warned by teachers that they might need to "move down" to one of the other groupings. The imperative of autonomy, in other words, became an organizing logic in the school—a standard against which students and teachers came to assess practices and performance in its classrooms.

IMAGINATIVE INFRASTRUCTURES AND EDUCATIONAL EQUITY

The imagination is a powerful thing. The ways districts, schools, and teachers imagine innovative education creates infrastructures that discipline what kind of learning manifests. This should not be controversial. As institutions invested in young people's formation and growth, schools are not just in the business of defining and delimiting what students ought to *know*, but what they ought to *be*. Nothing experienced by students in schools is impartial, unbiased, or apolitical. Educators have a responsibility to interrogate the imagined ideals that drive the norms and practices that are nurtured or suppressed in classrooms. This is especially true when those imperatives seem neutral or universally agreed-upon. If some disposition or practice feels intuitively good or right, deviations from this norm (and those doing the deviating) become the opposite—even if these departures are legitimate and principled. Attending to these imaginative infrastructures, then, has important implications for educational equity.

As we have seen, many students at the Innovation School had good reasons to strive for or stray from the imperatives of autonomy. Some, like Crystal, viewed it as an opening for sharing and spreading her ideas, while students like Devi saw it as secondary to his interest in other forms of innovative education (e.g., technology). Still others, like Kalif, remained unclear about what was expected from his content-area learning. Viewed from the standpoint of innovation from below, we can recognize these alignments and tensions as outgrowths of imaginaries converging and competing in the classroom. However, within the logic of the linear model, it is far easier to conflate students' confusions, hesitations, and alternate priorities as individual shortcomings—failures to adapt to the "innovative" imperatives of the school. We see this reflected in the way students were positioned in the first year as "getting" or "not getting" the school model. These designations ultimately congealed by the second year into a classification system based on student autonomy. Even though teachers and research team members were committed to caring and equitable learning, and repeatedly reinforced that these autonomy groupings were not based on ability, the linear model persisted in reasserting them as a hierarchy. Some kids would have to be left behind for innovation to persist.

This tiering had uneven impacts on students. Those who shared the innovation imaginary of the school were able to thrive in its classrooms. Those who did not were grouped in a manner that suggested their misalignments were the result of a lack of autonomy. In other words, they were clustered by a deficit orientation. Yet it was not even clear exactly what this "autonomy deficiency" actually meant in the school context. Indeed, we can see a great deal of autonomy in the playful and strategic subversions that students devised to navigate the unfamiliar conditions of the innovative classroom. Leveraging competency-based projects to avoid boring, computer-based lessons and finding workarounds to retake quizzes could certainly be regarded as innovative agency. We might also find autonomy in Devi's decision not to engage in a project until he saw a purpose that aligned with his own ideas about innovative learning. Similarly, Kalif's reluctance to commit to an assignment when it was unclear how he would be evaluated was a legitimate expression of his autonomy. In these senses, while the imperatives of the school were oriented toward "autonomy," in practice, the expectation was for students to perform "autonomy" in a narrow and specific sense of the term. Autonomy had to be productive in a way that was legible to the school model's vision of innovative education.

In highlighting these asymmetries, my purpose is not to point out flaws in the teachers' or district's innovation imaginaries, or to critique their pedagogical choices. In fact, their ideas and practices had much in common with my own and those of other members of the research team during the partnership. Rather, I bring up these asymmetries in autonomy to demonstrate how the linear model of innovation sets the conditions of possibility for these imaginaries. In the process, it makes the confusions, breakdowns, and inequities that result difficult to avoid. By prioritizing intuitive ideas about innovation, the linear model stacks the deck in favor of those who share those tacit understandings and against those who might question why their own conceptions of innovation have been discounted. While we have focused on autonomy in this chapter, this analysis could also be extended to the long list of seemingly intuitive ideals that students are increasingly being measured against in schools, like grit, resilience, creativity, a growth mindset, and critical thinking. Attending to the imaginative infrastructures of such ideals helps to reveal the imperatives that drive them, and to create space for interrogating who they serve. With this in mind, this chapter has created the possibility for alternate imaginaries—including those that have historically been marginalized in dominant school structures—to be folded into classrooms in ways that might reconfigure the priorities of innovation in the service of helping students and communities flourish.

CHAPTER 2

Pedagogical Infrastructures

It's a Tuesday afternoon early in the Innovation School's second year. In the Community Organizing Makerspace, students are meeting with members of a local activist group that fights for affordable housing in nearby neighborhoods. The students will use the insights they glean from the meeting as the foundation of an oral history project, in which they will interview recent- and long-term residents to understand changes in the school's surrounding community over time. They are entranced by the speakers. As the activists speak, students excitedly ask questions and draw parallels to their own experiences on their own blocks. In the back of the room, I check to make sure my audio recorder is capturing the scene—only to discover that the battery has died, predictably at the most interesting moment.

Careful not to disrupt the flow of the dialogue, I slip out a side door and hurry down the hall to an unused classroom where our research team stores equipment and materials. I grab my backup audio recorder and turn to leave but pause when I hear a sound coming from the large coat closet at the end of the room. Pulling open the door, I am surprised to see Nadia, a second-year student, sitting on the closet floor while typing on her Chromebook. I ask why she is in the closet, and she explains this is where she comes to work on her humanities assignments. Her humanities class was recently restructured in the image of the school's makerspaces. She said she found it lively and fun, but the humming environment made it difficult for her to concentrate. She needed quiet and calm to make sense of assigned passages and project guidelines. In moments when she had trouble focusing, Nadia would ask to go to the bathroom and then hide here, in the tranquility of her "study closet."

After my encounter with Nadia, I asked other students about their experiences in the Humanities Makerspace. I quickly learned that she was not the only one who sometimes found it difficult to concentrate in the chaotic atmosphere. Nor was she alone in inventing clever counterstrategies to work around the noise. Some students pulled chairs into the quiet hallway outside the makerspace. Others, like Nadia, made use of the large coat closets in different classrooms; the closet in the science lab, which was more spacious than the others, was a particular favorite. Students who had not found such refuges often opted to use their class time for activities that required less concentration, like planning unit projects, talking with friends, and watching YouTube videos. They saved the more demanding reading and writing to do at home, where there were fewer distractions. But not everyone was bothered, or only bothered, by the buzz of the makerspace. Many, including students who had difficulty focusing in the room, also found inspiration in the energy and excitement of students taking ownership of their learning. They enjoyed seeing classmates creating projects that might not have been welcomed, much less encouraged, in the schools they attended before coming to the Innovation School.

The teachers in the Humanities Makerspace were aware of students' mixed reactions to the class. In planning meetings and after-school conversations, they wrestled with how to make sense of them. Was the Humanities Makerspace working? Was it effective, as an innovation? Should it be continued? Adapted? Abandoned? There wasn't a single or simple answer to such questions. Much like we saw in the last chapter, what seemed to work well for some created new challenges and obstacles for others. This unevenness is a persistent challenge in evaluating the success of innovations, educational and otherwise. It would be comforting if we could easily categorize teaching innovations as good or bad, effective or ineffective, just or unjust. In reality, they are usually a muddy mixture of both. Media theorist and educator Neil Postman (1992) suggests that innovations always create both winners and losers, those who gain stability or advantage from some new device, technique, or strategy, and those who lose it. When determining whether to move forward with or abandon a given innovation it often comes down to a cruel calculus: Exactly how many (and which) people can be made losers before the cost begins to outweigh the benefit to the winners? In this chapter, I argue that there is another way of understanding and evaluating innovations than as a cost-benefit analysis—one focused not on *if*, but *how*, innovations work in practice.

Rather than looking to external markers of success (e.g., classroom productivity, improved assessment scores, or students' enjoyment), this orientation examines how innovations transform the underlying relations of classrooms that condition how teaching and learning unfold. We can call these relations *pedagogical infrastructures*. Using the example of the Humanities Makerspace, we'll explore how innovations that were intended to alter one form of pedagogical infrastructure often have ripple effects on others, leading to uneven and unexpected impacts for the teachers and the students who depend on them to learn. Ultimately, I suggest that addressing the frictions that surface when pedagogical infrastructures are reconfigured allows educators to forego the usual cost-benefit analysis approach to weighing the merits of a given innovation. Instead, being attentive to pedagogical infrastructures opens educators to a wider repertoire of resources for identifying, responding to, and preventing inequities in schools.

PEDAGOGY AS INFRASTRUCTURE

The term *pedagogical infrastructure* can sound a bit complicated, but it's really just giving language to an idea that many educators are already intuitively aware of. When we think about good pedagogy, we probably don't envision a direct and unmediated transfer of knowledge from the mind of a teacher to the mind of student. *Star Trek* aside, education is not simply a Vulcan mind meld. More likely, we think about the arrangement of the classroom environment, the form that instruction takes, and the interactions and routines that allow students to meaningfully engage with the content and interact with other participants in the class. In other words, what comes to mind are the *supports* that nurture and sustain learning over time. Pedagogical infrastructure is another name for these supports.

In my research on educational innovation and experience at the Innovation School, I've found that most innovations in teaching and learning tend to focus on five broad forms of infrastructure: physical, spatial, curricular, communicative, and administrative. Let's take a closer look at each.

Physical Infrastructure

I start with physical infrastructure because it tends to be what people most commonly think of as infrastructure, and it serves as a foundation for other pedagogical infrastructures. This form of infrastructure includes the physical materials, resources, and services that undergird the activities of schools. Physical infrastructure affects the condition of the building and its classrooms, and the functioning of its basic utilities—water, electricity, heating, cooling, and Internet connectivity. Infrastructures like these are often so necessary that they can fade into the background. Most teachers and students don't really think much about them until they break down. When the air conditioning malfunctions on a sweltering day, or the wireless Internet crashes during an online activity, we become acutely aware of just how important they are as pedagogical infrastructures.

Spatial Infrastructure

Like physical infrastructure, spatial infrastructure is also related to the school and classroom environment, but is focused more on spatial arrangement and organization. When teachers divide their classroom so that students can move freely between different zones of activity, or they configure desks and tables to better facilitate peer-to-peer collaboration, they are designing a spatial infrastructure aligned with their larger pedagogical aims. Crucially, spatial infrastructures can be better for supporting some activities and worse for others. The spatial infrastructure for a hands-on science lab, for instance, might be a lousy infrastructure for a creative writing class, and vice versa. Effective spatial infrastructure often requires tuning of a class-room environment to the goals of particular teachers and needs of particular students.

Curricular Infrastructure

Curricular infrastructure refers to the sequencing and ordering of course content. It is what students actually do (and, by extension, learn) in a lesson, unit, or class. Curricular infrastructure can range from the hyper-regimented to the almost entirely unstructured. When I was in high school, for instance, my math teacher assigned one section of the textbook each day, and gave the class a test when we reached the end of a chapter. This is markedly dif-ferent from educators who use "backward design" (Wiggins & McTighe, 1998) to organize courses and units around essential questions and plan successions of activities that allow students to explore and answer them. This approach is different still from forms of unschooling, deschooling, and play-based learning that resist prescribing curricular content that doesn't arise from students' interests (Jones et al., 2015). How much freedom teach-ers have to set or adapt the curricular infrastructure of their classroom also depends on the school, district, surrounding community, and their personal levels of comfort and experience.

Communicative Infrastructure

The communicative infrastructure of a classroom includes the ways that interactions among teachers, students, and the curriculum are mediated. When an educator elects to share information with students through a read-ing rather than a video or lecture or podcast, they are making a choice about what kinds of communicative infrastructures students use to encounter that material. Instructional technologies are one of the most common forms of communicative infrastructure. Whiteboards, smartboards, content manage-ment systems (e.g., Class Dojo, Google Classroom), and interactive apps are all means of conditioning how students engage with course content, their teachers, and each other. Opportunities for paired learning, small-group conversations, and whole-class discussions are also communicative infra-structure. In this way, the combinations of communicative infrastructure at work in a given context, even simultaneously, can be fairly expansive. We will also see that communication creates both opportunities and challenges when these infrastructures are "disrupted" by a new innovation.

Administrative Infrastructure

The final form of infrastructure, administrative infrastructure, is concerned with the noncurricular routines, rituals, and procedures that support teaching and learning in schools. This can include schoolwide policies that promote inclusive practices, and disciplinary protocols that encourage restorative justice rather than punitive measures. Much like physical infrastructures, administrative supports can easily fade into the background when they are working well; and they can just as easily undermine other forms of infrastructure when they aren't. A discriminatory or invasive school disciplinary policy, for example, can quickly undo the efforts of individual teachers to show care for their students and make them feel welcome.

INTEROPERABILITY

When we step back and look across these forms of pedagogical infrastructure, we can begin to recognize something important about the way "innovation" is invoked in school reform efforts. Most of the time, when a corporation, philanthropy, consultant, politician, or edupreneur marches out a shiny innovative fix for education, they are prioritizing the "disruption" of one of these pedagogical infrastructures to drive system-wide transformation. Tech firms, for instance, may spotlight schools' communicative infrastructures as ripe for reform. Familiar teacher–student interactions, they might say, are outdated and inefficient, but data-driven and automated services (the kind they happen to sell for convenient rates in auto-renewable subscriptions) can streamline instruction and learning. We can see parallel claims made about other forms of pedagogical infrastructure throughout history.

In the 1960s, advocates of open classrooms believed that altering the spatial infrastructure of schools would revolutionize education. They removed walls between classes and created common areas for young people to congregate and collaborate. "No Excuses" charter programs emphasize rigid administrative and curricular infrastructures that center order and compliance as foundations for improved student performance on standardized tests. Indeed, we can even understand the decades-long creep of privatization into public education as an effort to "disrupt" education's ties to physical infrastructure altogether. School takeovers, the shuttering and selling of buildings, and the growth of platform-based "cyber learning" question whether school sites should be invested in at all as a public commons (Ewing, 2018; Schneider & Berkshire, 2020).

Diverse as these reform priorities are, they are rooted in a shared assumption: that educational innovation begins with identifying, targeting, and changing one form of pedagogical infrastructure *in isolation* from the others. The allure of this view is obvious. It would certainly be convenient if coherent, systemic transformation was simply a matter of exchanging an old or faulty part with a new or working one. But the reality of educational transformation is more complicated than replacing a battery or installing a software update. Pedagogical infrastructures aren't amenable to singular, independent fixes because they are fundamentally *multiple* and *interdependent*. Any significant change—large or small, predictable or unpredictable, positive or negative—to one form of pedagogical infrastructure will have ripple effects in others. Anthropologists Susan Leigh Star and Karen Ruhleder (1996) refer to the relationships between different forms of infrastructure as their "interoperability." That is, even though infrastructures exist as distinct categories, they always *interoperate*—working with or against each other. Figure 2.1 offers a visualization of these relations among pedagogical infrastructures. An interoperable perspective on pedagogical infrastructure can help clarify why educational innovations so often fall short of their promises. By centering one form of infrastructure as the key to systemic transformation, they overlook interoperability. The relations *between* and *among* infrastructures are far more significant in shaping how, for whom, and to what extent an innovation works in practice.

Figure 2.1. Visualization of Interactions Among Pedagogical infrastructures

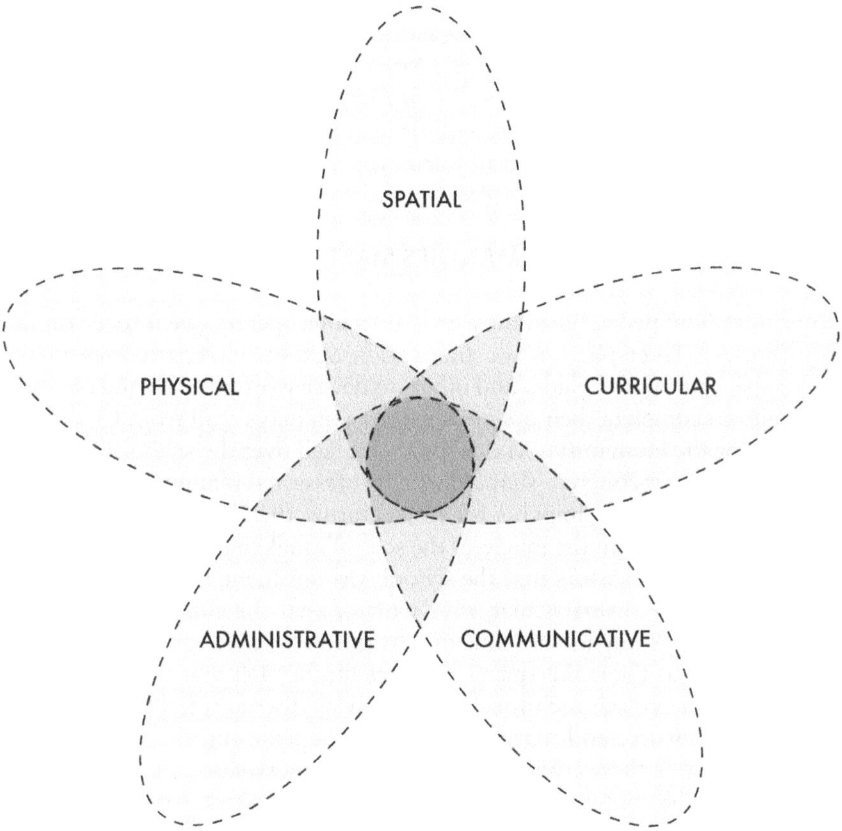

Interoperability is so important because, as we saw in the last chapter, infrastructures are not always compatible with one another—and even when they are, their combination can lead to unexpected results. Just as different imaginative infrastructures, each driven by a competing interest, can lead to frustrations when they are layered together in schools, pedagogical infrastructures can also be combative. In fact, they are often antagonistic, since they are products of diverse innovation imaginaries, and they tend to accumulate, combine, and multiply over time (Jackson et al., 2007). The plurality of pedagogical infrastructures at work in a given school leaves open innumerable opportunities for incompatibilities to surface and for breakdowns to occur.

If you've spent time in a classroom, you've almost certainly experienced one of these breakdowns. Maybe your presentation ground to a halt from an Internet outage, an administrative policy was disconnected from the realities of practice, or a teaching technique left students more confused than enlightened. Maddening as they can be, such moments offer an important resource for understanding how interoperability works. As Star and Ruhleder (1996) suggest, it is often in instances of tension and breakdown—or *frictions*, as I will call them—that the invisible operations of infrastructures become visible to us (cf. Edwards et al., 2009). Attending to the frictions that arise in practice, then, can give educators insight into how a classroom's pedagogical infrastructures are working with or against one another, and what this means for equitable teaching and learning.

THE HUMANITIES MAKERSPACE

To explore how pedagogical infrastructures interoperate, we'll focus on the Humanities Makerspace in the Innovation School. Here, frictions in the makerspace prompted Nadia and others to devise workarounds and counter-strategies to complete their assignments. As you may recall from Chapter 1, the idea for the Humanities Makerspace emerged over the school's first year and began taking concrete shape during professional planning the summer before its second. The impetus for restructuring the Humanities and other content-area classes in the image of the school's makerspaces was a growing concern among educators that the school was not living up to the "innovation" in its name. In particular, they worried that the content-area classes weren't offering students the same opportunities for asynchronous, autonomous learning as the makerspaces. As a result, they felt that students might, over time, come to see such forms of inquiry as disconnected from the core humanities, science, and math curriculum. The solution, they determined, was to reimagine these courses themselves as makerspaces.

Of all of the content-area instructors, the humanities teachers were the most enthusiastic supporters of the transformation. I admit, this initially surprised me. Since making and makerspaces frequently get associated with STEM education, I'd assumed the science and math teachers would be the most energized to incorporate them into their classrooms. However, in talking with the humanities teachers and sitting in on their summer planning, I began to understand their attraction to the makerspace model. To them, the organization and practices of makerspaces aligned with several already-existing innovations in humanities education that were central to their own teaching.

One such alignment was a concern with process. The humanities teachers often stressed to students that writing is about "process, not product." Building on earlier, process-based writing pedagogics (Murray, 1972), they taught their classes to engage in recursive cycles of planning, drafting, and revising, conferring with students periodically to provide feedback and support. In the makerspaces, the teachers saw a similar orientation: Making wasn't about creating a product, but about participating in an iterative and emergent design process. These commonalities suggested to them that the two could be generatively combined.

A second area of alignment was how time and space were used in makerspaces. Compared to more conventional classrooms, time in the school's makerspaces was mostly unstructured. There was minimal (if any) interaction that simultaneously engaged the whole class. Instead, students moved between independent and collaborative activity zones as they worked on projects, pausing periodically for targeted, small-group minilessons and one-on-one check-ins with their teacher. While this was not how the humanities teachers facilitated their classrooms in the school's first year, they recognized a structural resemblance to familiar reading and writing workshop models that they admired (Atwell, 1987). Though there is variation in how such workshops are organized, they commonly involve decentering whole-class, teacher-led activities in favor of targeted, small-group lessons that provide ample time for students' independent work (Graham & Perin, 2007). In this way, the humanities teachers saw makerspaces not just as a new innovation to implement, but as an extension of already-existing innovations that they understood to be in alignment with their own pedagogical goals.

These humanities teachers were not alone in seeing resonances between making and humanities education. As early as 2013, the National Writing Project—a large professional learning network focused on literacy education, often from a process- and workshop-based orientation (Whitney & Friedrich, 2013)—was offering "writing as making" professional development seminars (National Writing Project, 2013). In recent years, a growing research base has begun to conceptualize "maker literacies" as a frame for understanding the role of making and makerspaces in literacy and civic learning (Marsh et al., 2018; McLean & Rowsell, 2021). Such developments highlight a more general enthusiasm for using making in humanities teaching and learning. But perceiving synergies between an innovation and an existing practice isn't the same as actually integrating them.

(RE-)MAKING INFRASTRUCTURES

As the humanities teachers soon discovered, merging making and the humanities would require them to embed the pedagogical infrastructures of makerspaces into the infrastructures already at work in their classrooms. This was no simple task. In places where these infrastructures weren't exactly aligned, their incongruities would need to be reconciled. In other words, the teachers would need to choose which supports from their existing classrooms would remain, and which would be remade to accommodate the imperatives of the makerspace, as an innovation.

As the teachers worked to transform their humanities classrooms into Humanities Makerspaces, three forms of pedagogical infrastructure emerged as the focus of their efforts: the curricular, the communicative, and the spatial. Because, as we have noted, these infrastructures are interdependent, changes in one affected the others. In this way, the transformation was not an additive process (i.e., the old humanities classroom plus making), but an ecological one. It required creating an entirely new classroom environment with its own unique configuration of pedagogical infrastructures. To understand this environment, we can look to the infrastructural shifts that drove its formation.

Curricular

In the Innovation School's first year, the curricular infrastructure for the humanities classes largely followed a "backward design" model (Wiggins & McTighe, 1998). A widely-used approach to curriculum, backward design involves organizing units around guiding questions, and then working backward (hence the name) to create lessons and assignments that gradually lead students to provisional answers that deepen their understandings. Most often, these scaffolding activities are aligned to specific content-area standards or competencies that are to be taught throughout the school year. For instance, in a unit focused on the question "What is Identity?," the humanities classes read poetry, short stories, and narrative nonfiction. Through reading, they explored different forms and expressions of identity, and considered the significance of identity in historical and current events. They then wrote essays to synthesize what they had learned and to make connections to their own lives. Throughout this process, students could earn competencies for literary and historical analysis as well as expository writing.

As the first year ended, the humanities teachers weighed how to make their classes more like the school's makerspaces. They didn't want to abandon "backward design" altogether. For the most part, they saw the inquiry-based units as successful. What was missing—and what the makerspaces seemed to offer—was greater student control over learning. While backward design provided flexibility for diverse engagements within the curriculum, lessons were still largely synchronous, whole-class activities facilitated by adults. They thought that turning the humanities class into a makerspace would mean restructuring the curriculum so that it could be completed non-linearly, at each student's own pace, and without the direct guidance of a teacher.

To accomplish this, the humanities team took inspiration from "the design process," a five-stage framework that was used to guide activities in the school's makerspaces (Figure 2.2). Based on similar models that use "design thinking" as a guide for students to infuse out-of-school interests and expertise into school projects (e.g., Genius Hour, Passion Projects, 20 Percent Time; cf. Juliani, 2014; Wettrick, 2014), the Innovation School's Design Process moved students through an iterative sequence for researching (Discover/Define), imagining (Design), prototyping (Develop), and sharing (Deliver) projects. As we have already noted, the humanities teachers saw in this recursive model echoes of the writing process they emphasized in their own instruction. But even more significantly, as they contemplated the role that making might play in their classes, they also began to see the design process framework as a model for reorganizing the entire curriculum.

Following this idea, the teachers began reformulating their courses. They started by merging their thematically focused "backward design" units with the iterative structure of "the design process." Each unit retained a guiding question, but now the activities that scaffolded students' engagement with it were organized according to the stage of the design process with which they aligned (Table 2.1). For example, "Discover" activities framed the unit's overarching inquiry, immersing students in its central tensions and themes. "Define" activities introduced or reinforced concepts and vocabulary that would support students in completing the unit project. "Design" and "Develop" activities involved drafting, prototyping, and soliciting feedback on an open-ended project that addressed the unit theme. Finally, "Deliver" activities invited students to share their work with the class or other public audiences. Importantly, because the stages of the design process were meant to be nonlinear and recursive, the teachers stressed that

Figure 2.2. The Innovation School's Design Process

Table 2.1. Example of a "playlist" for a unit on American Mythology. Activities are organized according to the stage of the design process with which they aligned.

Student Activities	Practice or Mastery	Time to Complete	Goal Date	Completed Date
Discover				
1.01 Journal response: What are "American myths"	Practice	20–40 mins		
1.02 Competency self-assessment: Historical narrative/ myth	Practice	20–40 mins		
1.03 Notes: Introduction of the Life Story of Hamilton	Practice	45–90 mins		
Mini-lesson: Understanding the Burr–Hamilton Duel (Close Reading)	Practice	10–15 mins		
1.04 HOT Task: About Mythic America (cite evidence, author's purpose, central idea)	Mastery (ELA 2.1, 2.2)	90–120 mins		
Define				
1.05 Vocabulary: America's Mythology	Mastery (ELA 2.9)	45–90 mins		
1.06 HOT Task: Cite evidence to support your interpretation of "My Shot"	Mastery (ELA 2.1)	45–90 mins		
Design				
1.07 Performance Task: Determine a topic of Your American Myth	Practice	45–90 mins		
Mini-lesson: Plot mapping (using facts and fiction)	Practice			
1.08 Performance Task: Your American Myth plot map	Practice	45–90 mins		
1.09 Performance Task: Draft an exposition that orients your reader in the opening of your myth	Mastery (ELA 5.1)	60–120 mins		

(*continued*)

Student Activities	Practice or Mastery	Time to Complete	Goal Date	Completed Date
1.10 Performance Task: Draft the rising action and build tension to a climax using facts and fiction	Mastery (ELA 5.2)	60–120 mins		
1.11 Performance Task: Draft the falling action and resolution. What values will readers learn from this American Myth?	Mastery (ELA 5.5)	60–120 mins		
Develop				
1.12 First Draft of Your American Myth	Mastery (ELA 5.3, 5.7)	60–120 mins		
1.13 Peer Revision of Your American Myth	Mastery (ELA 5.6)	45–90 mins		
Deliver				
1.14 Best Draft of Your American Myth: Revise and Submit	Mastery (5.1–5.8)	60–120 mins		
Mini-lesson: American Myth Story Slams—Public Presentation	Practice	20–45 mins		
1.15 End of Unit Reflection	Mastery (HOS)			

these activities need not be completed sequentially. A student might begin in the "Design" stage, for instance, and then move to the "Discover" and "Define" stages at a moment when it would be most useful to their creative process. This was one reason why they referred to the catalog of activities that made up each unit as a "playlist" (see Chapter 1); to get to the end, it could be completed in order or shuffled.

Communicative

For students to navigate this new curricular infrastructure, the communicative infrastructure of the humanities classrooms would also have to evolve. On a given day in the school's first year, the communicative infrastructure followed a fairly straightforward pattern: The teacher would greet students at the door, provide context and direction for the day's activities, and then circulate throughout the room to offer guidance or feedback as students worked. There were other communicative infrastructures in play as well, like student laptops, cellphones, books and magazines, handouts and note sheets. But it was still the teachers' moderating voice and presence that guided the class through the synchronous activities of lessons and units. While it was often effective, the teacher-centeredness of this arrangement concerned the humanities team. After all, the more dependent students were on the teacher, the less autonomy they had in their own learning. In this way, transforming the humanities classroom into a Humanities Makerspace would require not just a curriculum that students could complete asynchronously, but communicative infrastructures to support them in doing so.

Because the new curriculum would be nonlinear, students in the Humanities Makerspace would no longer encounter lessons and activities together. There would need to be a way for them to move through unit playlists without the teacher giving them explicit instructions. To accomplish this, the teachers devised a communicative shift: Rather than offering direction to all students at the start of a class, details about each assignment—the task, where it fit in relation to larger unit inquiry, and how it would be assessed—would be written out for students to read and use as needed. In other words, what was previously spoken would become *textualized*. For each activity on a unit playlist, the teachers created a coversheet that replicated the information they previously shared with students to frame daily activities or to redirect them during class time (Table 2.2). This textualization, they believed, would give students control over the pace at which they worked through the asynchronous curriculum. But the shift also created a new challenge.

With everyone working on different assignments at their own pace, how could teachers provide support, feedback, and encouragement on so many independent student trajectories? The forms of teacher–student interaction that worked in the school's first year were not nearly flexible enough to accommodate the variety and fluidity of activities in a makerspace. For this reason, the communicative infrastructure for student support would also need to be remade. To do so, the humanities team reflected on what the work of teaching ought to look like in an asynchronous classroom. Now that much of their routine instructional responsibilities were textualized, they determined their class time could be entirely reallocated to personal interactions with students. They created three categories for teacher–student communication: (1) *tune-ups*, 5-minute check-ins about specific problems students encountered while working through a playlist; (2) *minilessons*, 15-minute, teacher-led activities that introduced or reinforced targeted competencies from a unit in a small-group setting; and (3) *conferences*, 10-minute one-on-one meetings with students about their progress and growth. In a 75-minute class block, teachers would plan 1–2 minilessons and conferences and 5–10

Table 2.2. Example of a lesson coversheet, with textualized instructions

2.05 : HOT Task (ELA 2.1 & 2.2)
Determine Central Idea & Use Evidence to Support Explanation

Directions: Read and annotate the article, "5 Reasons to Vote (Even If You Hate Everything on the Ballot)" (2.05: Close Reading and Annotation). Identify three central ideas; track the developments of the central ideas and write a summary discussing the author's purpose and how the author responds to conflicting evidence (ELA 2.2). Then, discuss your opinion about the author's claim, and support your response using evidence (ELA 2.1).

As you prepare for this activity, it would be helpful to look back at your feedback for ELA 2.1 (1.06) and ELA 2.2 (1.04) to help you see what you need to focus on in this response. You must complete the text annotation before writing your response. Then, use the graphic organizer and sentence starters (2.05: Graphic Organizer) to help you construct your response (if necessary). If you're ready to write, check the prompt on the next page and dive in.

I will only grade the response in this page. Feel free to use additional lined paper, if necessary.

	Level 6	Level 7	Level 8	Level 10	Level 12
How well do I use evidence to support my interpretation of the text? (ELA 2.1)	I can cite one piece of evidence to support what the text says. I can cite one piece of evidence to support my opinion about the text.	I can cite three pieces of evidence to support what the text says. I can cite three pieces of evidence to support my opinion about the text.	I can cite three pieces of evidence and explain why they support what the text says. I can cite three pieces of evidence and explain why they support my opinion about the text.	I can cite and explain how multiple pieces of evidence support both what the text says and my opinion about it. I can explain why the evidence I selected is better than other valid pieces of evidence from the text.	I can cite and explain how multiple pieces of evidence support both what the text says and my opinion about it. I can identify other valid pieces of evidence and explain why my evidence is better. I can identify and explain places where the text contradicts itself or does not support my opinion about it.
How well can I analyze the author's purpose? (ELA 2.2)	I can identify the main idea or claim of a text and one detail that supports it; I can summarize what the text says.	I can identify the main idea or claim of a text. I can identify specific details that support the main idea or claim. I can summarize what the text says.	I can identify the main idea or claim of a text. I can identify specific details and explain how they support the main idea or claim. I can summarize what the text says.	I can identify multiple ideas or claims of a text. I can identify specific details and explain how they support each idea or claim. I can identify the author's response to conflicting claims and evidence. I can summarize what the text says.	I can identify multiple ideas or claims of a text and the details that support them. I can identify the thesis that all claims and ideas jointly form. I can identify and evaluate an author's response to other conflicting claims and evidence. I can summarize what the text says.

49

Table 2.3. Weekly planning template that teachers used to meet with students

	Class Section:			
	Mini-Lessons		Tune-Ups	Conferences
Day	Topic (+ link to lesson)	Students	Student (Topic)	Students
Mon				
Tues				
Wed				
Thurs				
Fri				

tune-ups each day. In lieu of formal, weekly lesson plans, they filled in a planning template to ensure they met with each student in one or more of these settings each week (Table 2.3). This communicative infrastructure would let the teachers support students without impeding their momentum in the classroom makerspace.

Spatial

These changes in the curricular and communicative infrastructures would also require space to be reconfigured. During the school's first year, the arrangement of the humanities classroom reflected the kinds of activities that most commonly occurred in them. Long tables were placed in a large U-shape, which allowed students to see one another during whole-class discussions. The seats all faced the front of the room, where the teacher delivered directions for the day's lesson. And there was space in this setup for the teacher to move around the inside of the U-shape to address questions and confusions that arose from students' synchronous independent work (Figure 2.3). While this spatial infrastructure seemed appropriate for these forms of activity, the humanities team knew it was insufficient to support the bustle of student-directed, asynchronous learning.

The teachers began reimagining classroom space to accommodate the anticipated shifts in their curriculum and communicative practices. Together, they sketched a mockup of the new Humanities Makerspace (Figure 2.4). The U-shaped table configuration was replaced with decentralized "work zones" that students could move between, as their sequenced playlist and their creative process demanded. The "Independent Work Zone" included tables for quiet, individual study. The "Collaborative Work Zone" designated seating for small groups that were partnering on assignments or projects. The "Minilesson Work Zone" revived the U-shaped tables in a space where the teacher could deliver short bursts of targeted instruction.

Figure 2.3. The humanities classroom during the school's first year.

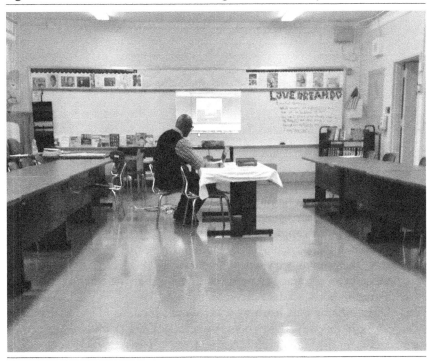

Figure 2.4. Recreation of the teachers' mockup for the design of the Humanities Makerspace

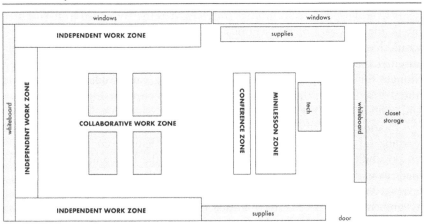

Figure 2.5. The Actual Humanities Makerspace

Finally, the "Conference Work Zone" was simply a table and chairs where the teacher could hold one-on-one meetings with students.

As the second year began, and the teachers' mock-up materialized as a living learning environment, these supports not only accommodated the parallel shifts in the curricular and communicative infrastructures, but also introduced their own pedagogical imperatives (Figure 2.5). Each space was designed to encourage patterns of activity that the teachers associated with autonomous, student-driven education. Indeed, in each zone, they hung signs outlining how learning was to look, sound, and feel in that area (Figure 2.6). In this way, these zones emerged as a new spatial infrastructure for pedagogy in the humanities classroom.

MAKING FRICTIONS

These changes to the pedagogical infrastructures transformed the humanities classroom into an altogether new learning environment, one that students would need to acculturate themselves to as they returned from summer break for the start of the school's second year. The teachers knew there would likely be growing pains as students learned to navigate the unfamiliar curricular, communicative, and spatial supports they'd devised. But they thought the challenges would be worth enduring; once students passed their initial discomforts, they'd be positioned to take ownership over the pace and content of their education.

In some ways, the teachers' vision for autonomous and self-motivated learning did come to fruition. Some students immediately recognized the powerful possibilities that the new infrastructures of the Humanities Makerspace made available. Miguel, a second-year student with a passion for filmmaking, leveraged the textualized communicative infrastructure to complete his playlist assignments at home. He freed himself from using class time for assignments to take advantage of the video cameras and editing software he didn't have access to outside of the school. During a unit focused on the 2016 election,

Figure 2.6. Teacher-created sign for identifying the qualities of the Independent Work Zone. Similar signs were posted in each of the makerspace's activity zones.

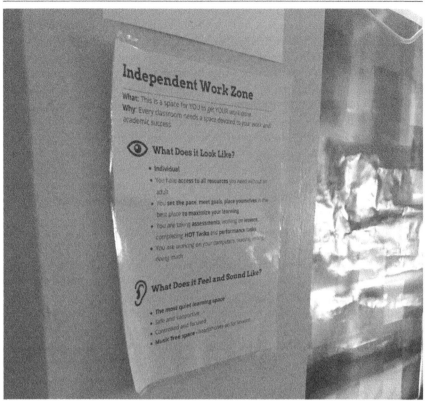

Miguel used the open-ended final project—creating a message to the future president—as an opportunity to combine his interest in film with his commitment to social justice. Moving through stages of the design process, he wrote a spoken-word poem about urban underdevelopment, calling out the complicity of the two-party system in privileging corporate interests over investments in communities of color. He then turned this poem into a short film, in which his delivery of the poem was punctuated with B-roll footage captured in gentrifying neighborhoods surrounding the school. This film was ultimately screened at a local festival. Later, it was elevated by the humanities teachers as an exemplar of how the makerspace model could cultivate richer forms of literacy and civic engagement than was possible in the previous classroom structure.

Miguel was not alone in seeing the pedagogical infrastructures of the Humanities Makerspace as an opportunity to do meaningful, self-directed work. Other students similarly used the design process and asynchronous class time to produce a range of creative projects inspired by their content-area learning. They created short stories, infographics, podcasts, and videos that explored complex and personal topics, ranging from mass incarceration to mental health (see Stornaiuolo & Nichols, 2018; Nichols & Johnston, 2020; Nichols et al., 2019). And yet, as powerful as these examples were, they didn't really reflect how the majority of students experienced the Humanities Makerspaces. As we saw at the start of this chapter, many students found the makerspace difficult to concentrate in. They found it disorienting enough that some would opt not to participate at all, while others, like Nadia, would seek out alternate spaces for quiet work.

While it would be possible to interpret these incongruities merely as transitional growing pains as students adapted to the new model, such explanations can prevent us from carefully considering the frictions that produce these uneven results. *Frictions* is the term I use for those moments when plans go awry—when a process that is supposed to flow smoothly starts to feel sticky or potholed, or the ideal of an imagined outcome bumps up against the realities of practice. As Star and Ruhleder (1996) suggest, it is often in such moments of friction that the invisible work of infrastructures is revealed. This is because frictions often arise in places where infrastructures are working against one another; in other words, where their interoperation is rough. Attending to these frictions, then, can shift our focus from *if* innovations are working (a question whose answer is almost always, unhelpfully, yes for some and no for others) to *how* they are working, for whom, and to what ends. This shift can attune us to infrastructural inequities, and potential avenues for alleviating them.

With this orientation, we can take a closer look at the Humanities Makerspace, and two forms of frictions that surfaced from shifts in its pedagogical supports: frictions *across* infrastructures and frictions *within* infrastructures.

Frictions Across Infrastructures

As the phrase suggests, "frictions across infrastructures" refers to tensions that surface as different types of supports interoperate with one another. The most obvious instances of these frictions occur when there is an overt incompatibility between categories of infrastructure. For instance, teachers might try to implement a new communicative shift when the physical infrastructure is lacking. As I write this, many teachers and students are experiencing this friction firsthand during the COVID-19 pandemic. Pivots to remote instruction on virtual communication platforms have been stymied by the absence of stable Internet (physical infrastructure) and a quiet working environment (spatial infrastructure) for many students. Frictions don't only emerge out of overt incompatibilities like these; they can also arise from compatibilities that change the experience of learning in ways that are jarring or unexpected for students. This is the more subtle and common form of friction across infrastructures. And it is what Nadia was experiencing that day I found her in her study-closet.

When I'd asked Nadia why she was working in the closet, her response was that she found it difficult to concentrate in the bustle of the Humanities Makerspace. Hearing this, it would be easy to conclude that the central challenge Nadia was running up against in the classroom was the noise and commotion. Indeed, as I talked to other students and heard similar accounts, this was how I initially understood the incongruity between the planned vision of the makerspace and how students were actually experiencing it. After discussing the matter with teachers, many of the solutions we devised focused on moderating the volume of noise in the room by creating norms for how to move, talk, and work respectfully. Only later did the teachers and research team members begin to see that these solutions were addressing a symptom rather than a cause of Nadia's problem. From an infrastructural view, the distractions that Nadia and others faced were not the problem. Nor could the problem be simply traced to students whose projects produced the noise, or whose work habits were ill-suited to the hum of the makerspace. At issue was a disconnect between the pedagogical infrastructures embedded in the classroom and the needs of students. The noise that drove students like Nadia to seek refuge elsewhere and others to disengage from coursework altogether was the observable friction that arose from this underlying mismatch.

This disconnect didn't emerge from one kind of infrastructure, but from the interoperation of several forms (Figure 2.7). The curricular infrastructure, for example, prioritized asynchronous, project-based activities, which meant that there was little uniformity in what students were working on in a given class period. The distractions generated from student work were only heightened by a spatial infrastructure that clustered independent work zones alongside areas for collaborative planning. Even when students would try to find a quiet space in the room, they were still close to small groups excitedly sharing ideas and creating projects. These challenges were also exacerbated by the communicative infrastructure of the makerspace. Because the instructions for assignments were being textualized in dense coversheets for each playlist activity, it was no longer being delivered and reinforced verbally by teachers. The result was an increased demand on students for focused reading even before they could begin work on an assignment. This was, understandably, a challenge for those who needed silence to concentrate.

Taken together, these factors created an environment rich in contradictions. Students were expected to move between focused independent work and lively collaborative deliberations in a space where both of these activities were happening simultaneously. For students like Miguel, who managed to navigate these tensions, the infrastructures that animated the

Figure 2.7. Frictions across infrastructures in the Humanities Makerspace

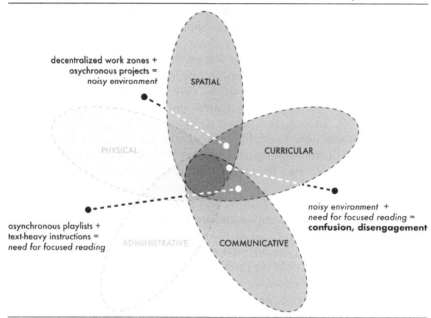

Humanities Makerspace offered powerful resources for inquiry-driven self-expression. For Nadia, these same infrastructures produced frictions that led students like her to seek out alternate spaces to make their way through the curriculum, and left others confused about the purpose or requirements of assignments in a given unit. Because the communicative infrastructure also divided teachers' one-on-one time with students each week, it was sometimes possible for questions to go unanswered for days before a tune-up or conference was scheduled.

Frictions Within Infrastructures

Shifts in the pedagogical supports in the Humanities Makerspace also surfaced a second form of friction: frictions within infrastructure. These types of frictions emerge when multiple innovations are consolidated in one type of pedagogical infrastructure. For instance, if a teacher implements a restorative justice approach to classroom discipline in a school whose overall administrative infrastructures are rigid and punitive, the competing logics work against one another. The clash between punishment and restorative justice creates frictions for the educators and students, who must live in and navigate these contradictions. For as often as innovations are advertised or celebrated as "disruptions" of the past, the truth is that they are deeply entwined with what has come before them. Innovations are always implemented *somewhere*, and that somewhere is always populated by already-existing innovations. Some of the old innovations may be taken for granted and no longer even register to those who use and depend on them. Where the old and new converge, frictions within infrastructure are likely to surface. One such concerning friction in the Humanities Makerspace was the volume of incomplete assignments.

By the end of the school's second year, less than half of the students had completed even half of the competencies necessary to advance to the next grade. The distractions that grew from the frictions across infrastructures described above certainly contributed to this, but they didn't offer a full explanation. In end-of-year interviews, students described the challenges they faced in finishing their asynchronous coursework. While noise was a recurring theme, many also expressed frustrations with the lack of clarity in what it meant to complete a unit and earn competencies. Student confusion came as a surprise to teachers, since as we saw in Chapter 1, the competency-based grading system was intended to make assessment and evaluation more transparent to students. Where was students' confusion coming from? After teachers and the research team began reflecting on its source, we would discover a significant disconnect in the makerspace's curricular infrastructure.

For the humanities team, the makerspace's spatial infrastructure had seemed to be well-aligned with their values and practices. As I mentioned above, it shared overlaps with several already-existing innovations that resonated with teachers: a focus on process that accorded with their approach to teaching composition, and an organization of time and space that aligned with reading and writing workshop models that they admired. But these ostensible synergies made it understandably difficult to see some important incongruities. Most notably, we missed how "competency-based standards" and "the design process" interoperated within in new curricular infrastructure.

Competencies, on one hand, are skills or practices through which students are expected to demonstrate proficiency in across content-area courses. In the humanities classes, this meant there was an expectation that the curriculum would allow students to hone their abilities in reading, writing, and civic and historical reasoning. This is another way of saying that competencies are a curricular infrastructure driven by discipline-specific goals, thought patterns, and activities. The "design process," on the other hand, tends to be discipline-agnostic as it is used in education. Indeed, professional designers have considered this, as they draw distinctions between forms of "expert design" unique to particular technical fields (e.g., architecture, engineering, visual arts) and the forms of "diffuse design" that humans universally participate in when they make things (Cross, 2001; Manzini, 2015). The Innovation School's design process (much like the Stanford d.School model on which it was based) reflects this universalist orientation. Posters of the design process model (Figure 2.2) were hung in every classroom in the school as a reminder that design transcended disciplines. Ben, the school's principal, even explicitly articulated the dominance of the design process in one of the first faculty meetings after the school's opening: "Discover. Define. Design. Develop. Deliver. You can see this in everything. This is a process that is universal." He went on to explain how the model offered a common language for project-based learning across content areas, saying, "We're framing design in the steps of proposing a lab, making a graph, analyzing city maps—or writing, making a photo essay or film." The design process, in other words, functioned as a curricular infrastructure primarily oriented toward transdisciplinary creative production.

As a result, the shift in curricular infrastructure that accompanied the transformation of the humanities classroom into a makerspace brought an ambiguity: Was the project-based learning in the new class configuration primarily a means of rehearsing and demonstrating disciplinary knowledge and practices (as the competency-based standards designated)? Or was the making of such projects an end in itself (as the design process seemed to suggest)? How one answered this question could have very different bearings on what it meant to complete a unit. From the standpoint of competencies, a unit was finished when students could show proficiency in its associated content-area standards. However, from the standpoint of the design process, finishing a unit meant completing its associated project—which could be interpreted as rendering any competency-based assignments not explicitly related to the project irrelevant.

Elijah, a Black student, gamer, and aspiring scientist in the school's second cohort, was one of many affected by this contradiction. Upon seeing the project description for the unit on American Mythology, he was immediately inspired. Having played the game *Assassin's Creed,* which depicted an alternate history in which George Washington became king rather than president, Elijah wanted to extend this conceit in a written story. After scanning the playlist of competency-aligned assignments, he determined they were unrelated to the project he had in mind. Instead, he looked online for resources related to Washington's relation to slavery. Synthesizing his findings into a fictional narrative, he submitted the draft *The Darkness of George Washington.* He received positive feedback from his teacher, as well as competencies for research and character development. However, he was given an incomplete for the overall unit because he had not finished the competency-aligned Discover and Define category assignments on the playlist. This frustrated Elijah. For him, those assignments were busywork, and peripheral to the main purpose of the unit—completing the project. He saw little purpose in doing activities that were inconsequential for what he was making. "If I did the project, it makes no sense to turn these assignments in too," he said. "I'm not going to write each individual assignment when

I could just do the project. It doesn't make any sense to break things down into smaller pieces just to stretch out the unit."

Of course, to the teachers, these assignments were not "stretching out" the unit—they were supporting it. As more students skipped assignments in order to focus on projects, the educators grew concerned. In an interview at the end of the second year, Christopher, one of the humanities teachers, expressed his frustration by saying, "We have to get kids finishing things. I think that's been another of the biggest frustrations . . . is students seeing the value in a finished product, and in seeing something through to the end." But students like Elijah believed they *were* valuing the finished product by working on the final project rather than getting sidetracked with procedural assignments. In this way, despite the ostensible alignments that educators initially saw between makerspaces and their humanities classrooms, the competing curricular infrastructures of "competency-based standards" and "the design process" created subtle but significant frictions that impacted both teachers and students.

VIEWING FRICTIONS "FROM BELOW"

The transformation of the humanities classroom into a Humanities Makerspace offered significant insights into how "innovation" operates in schools. New practices, strategies, and technologies that may appear well-aligned with the interests and values of teachers and students can easily, in practice, introduce imperatives that confuse, complicate, and even undermine these ideals. As we have seen, the makerspace structure resonated with the humanities teachers' commitments to student autonomy, process-oriented learning, and workshop-based classroom models. Yet its integration into their classrooms yielded frictions with uneven implications for students. Viewed from the perspective of the linear model of innovation, it's easy to interpret these frictions as growing pains: the necessary yet unfortunate byproduct of "creative destruction" that burns away the old and familiar to make room for the new. In the linear model, frictions are things we endure (or ignore) lest we stand in the way of progress. However, this chapter has shown that this is not the only way we might understand them. "Innovation from below" invites us to see frictions infrastructurally, and to attend to the relations of pedagogical supports that give rise to and animate them.

Seeing frictions "from below" helps shift our attention from *if* innovations universally work, to *how* and *for whom* they work. On the surface, the Humanities Makerspace could easily appear to be both a success (for students like Miguel) and a failure (for students like Nadia and Elijah). This unevenness made it difficult for teachers and research team members to use cost-benefit analysis to determine whether to persist with the makerspace migration or change course from its initial design. But looking beneath this surface at the interoperation of the makerspace's pedagogical infrastructures offers clarity as to why such different outcomes might result from the same innovation. Putting into place the infrastructures to support the goals of asynchronous, project-based learning also had the ripple effect of reconfiguring or eliminating already-existing infrastructures in the classroom. This meant that students who were well positioned to navigate these infrastructural changes (or who managed to work around the contradictions they introduced) were able to thrive in the new makerspace environment. Miguel, for instance, completed any work that required quiet, focused attention at home and took advantage of the school's video editing resources during school hours. He avoided the frictions that other students experienced with the noise and disruptions of the classroom. Not everyone had Miguel's flexibility. Those with family or job responsibilities that limited the out-of-school time they could devote to such tasks, for instance, were forced either to find alternate workspaces in the school, take shortcuts on their assignments, or fall further and further behind in the self-paced curriculum. As one student who fell in this latter category put it, "It gets stressful. . . . It's not that the work is difficult. It's just, sometimes you have a hard time catching up."

Examples like this student's response show how attention to pedagogical infrastructures can help reveal systemic inequities that might otherwise go unnoticed. Indeed, many of these dynamics were not immediately visible to teachers or research team members. While the new communicative infrastructure of the makerspace gave teachers significantly more one-on-one time with students each week, the absence of whole-class dialogue meant that they encountered successes and failures as outgrowths of individual student efforts. Success was not encountered as class-wide and systematic, conditioned by the underlying pedagogical infrastructures. In planning meetings and afterschool debriefs, a common concern among teachers was the concern that students were "unfocused" and "off-task" in the makerspaces. There was, in other words, a recognition of the frictions present in the classroom, but not always of the infrastructures that produced them.

It was the teachers who worked most closely with students outside of core classes—in guidance and learning-support settings—who first began to talk about how the uneven outcomes in the makerspaces might stem from infrastructural issues. They recognized that the classroom model that was meant to promote student autonomy was also creating obstacles that made it difficult for some young people to learn. In a year-end interview, Kelly, one of the school's learning-support specialists, questioned whether the innovative aspirations of the school model were actually serving all students equitably:

I don't know if I feel like we're "innovative" anymore. I don't feel successful right now at the things we say we do, which is teaching kids to take responsibility for their own learning and do it in a way that's asynchronous and personalized. I feel like there's so many pieces that we claim to do, and we just miss it.

As someone who worked closely with students who sometimes struggled to fit into the school's innovative model, Kelly's perspective points to the close relationship between pedagogical infrastructures and educational equity. When innovations are grafted onto classrooms, they carry with them imperatives for new infrastructural arrangements. Even when these infrastructures may appear to align with the interests and values of teachers, the process of integrating them may remove or alter already-existing pedagogical infrastructures that students depend on. Incongruities like these remind us that, while the linear model of innovation may celebrate disruption of familiar and settled practices, there is no guarantee that the new routines that replace them will be more just or equitable. The only way to ensure this is by approaching innovation from a different vantage point: not as dropped in from above, but nurtured from below through care and attention to the pedagogical supports that will allow every student to thrive.

CHAPTER 3

Technological Infrastructures

It's a Monday morning, and as I step off the bus at the stop down the street from the school I hear someone calling out to me. "Yo, Dr. Phil!" A few weeks before, students had pieced together that my name and proximity to academia meant that I could (and, thus, should) share a title with the popular TV psychologist—an epiphany that brought them much amusement. They quickly began referring to our interactions, from informal chats before or after school to more formal check-ins about their assignments, as "counseling sessions" ("Hey, Dr. Phil—can I get a session after lunch?").

Turning toward the voice, I see it is Jade. She breaks from the friends she's walking to school with and approaches me, eagerly holding out her phone. Jade was part of a creative writing club I was running during lunchtime. Just a few days ago, we'd had a "session" to discuss her concerns about writer's block and how writers capture ideas and inspiration for their work. On her phone was an open Notes document filled with fragmentary phrases, couplets, and stanzas. Jade told me she'd started jotting down observations on a long subway ride over the weekend. By the end of the trip, those words started to mingle and match to form the foundations of a poem. She was excited to share her experience turning her stray thoughts into poetry. We agreed that she should open our club meeting later that day by showcasing her approach, in case it would be helpful for the other writers in the group.

When lunch arrived, however, a very different Jade showed up to the room where our club met. The enthusiasm that animated our conversation that morning was gone, and she told me she didn't feel like sharing with her peers today. She was frustrated because in class that morning, a tech issue had erased multiple days of work on her unit project. A specialized video app she'd downloaded, which had advanced filtering and effects, was not allowing her to export the movie she'd made for the assignment without upgrading to a costly premium version. Without an exported file, she had no way to submit the video for credit. Her teacher was sympathetic, but needed the file to be able to view, assess, and comment on Jade's work. The only path forward, it seemed, was for Jade to redo the project using different software. Understandably, she felt upset and defeated.

Looking back on these incidents, what strikes me is the contradictory role that technology played in mediating Jade's experiences that day. Her energy and enthusiasm in our morning exchange had emerged from her phone's capacities for on-the-go note-taking, which she could weave into her writing process. Jade's phone—even its simple Notes app—offered powerful opportunities for meaningful learning and creative expression. These same opportunities were also at work in her failed video project. Jade's phone allowed her to capture, edit, and filter footage to make a creative product, but with an important caveat: the software's inability to freely export files made it incompatible with the classroom setting in which it operated. The same technology, in other words, was both an enabling and a constraining force.

Seeing technology as a force that gives and takes runs counter to its common depiction in the linear model of innovation. According to this model, technological developments are an engine of social advancement. Whatever growing pains we might experience by adopting the latest devices, gadgets, or techniques are necessary to not impede the inexorable march of progress. What this view misses, and what Jade's experience shows, is that the meaning and value of a technology is deeply *situated*. The same smartphone that inspires creative expression in one context (through the notes app or versatile video-editing tools) can inhibit it in another (through the barriers between personal devices and the school's tech ecosystem). The difference between the two doesn't rest in the sophistication of the technology, but in its relation to the practices and settings in which it operates. Understanding technology, then, means attending to the infrastructures that link hardware and software to the situations where they are used, and therefore condition how (and for whom) they work.

This chapter explores these technological infrastructures, and the ways they uphold or upend opportunities for equitable learning in schools. Some readers might be wondering why, in a book about educational innovation, we are only now talking explicitly about technology. There is good reason for this delay. As this chapter will make clear, viewing technology from below involves examining not only the infrastructures that inform its design and use, but also their interoperation with other infrastructures—including those we have discussed in previous chapters. Approaching the subject in this way saves us from the common mistake of weighing a technology's merits in isolation. Rather than rushing to adopt a new device based on its promised upsides, we are now in a position to see how such promises align with the imaginative and pedagogical infrastructures already at work in schools. In turn, this awareness can equip us to assess the ways that technologies introduce interests and imperatives into classrooms that may support, or work against, the aims and values of educators and students.

TECHNO-OPTIMISM AND TECHNO-PESSIMISM

Before exploring these technological infrastructures, it will be helpful to step back for a moment to confront two common narratives that drive how technology gets talked about and implemented in schools. The first is the *techno-optimist* narrative. This is the view that human and technological progress go hand in hand. From the alphabet to the printing press to the personal computer, developments in technology, it is suggested, have been catalysts for social, cultural, and intellectual advancement—easing workloads, increasing access to resources, improving quality of life. To those holding this view, a person or institution that resists adapting to new technologies is standing in the way of progress by clinging to the status quo. Indeed, one of the easiest ways to spot this narrative in the wild is to listen for accusations that some common practice is outmoded and must be brought up to date with the changing world.

In education, one common instance of techno-optimism is when would-be reformers invoke the charge that schools are factory-like relics of the industrial age as a way to legitimize the cutting-edge alternative the speaker is offering. The mission statement for the XQ Super Schools Project, an experimental school network founded by Laurene Powell Jobs, uses this tactic: "We've gone from the Model T to the Tesla, and from the switchboard to the smartphone. Yet high school has remained frozen in time" (Rolph, 2017). Similar sentiments proliferate in the speeches of education thought-leaders across the ideological spectrum, from Secretaries of Education Arne Duncan (2010) and Betsy DeVos (2015) to Sir Ken Robinson (2006), whose TED Talk about how factory-like schools are destroying creativity has been viewed more than 70 million times. Even though historians have repeatedly debunked the idea that schools are antiquated and unchanging widget factories (Schneider, 2015; Watters, 2015), the charge persists in the popular imagination because it accords with the widespread belief in the techno-optimist narrative. Technology is remaking the world, the story goes, and schools that fail to adapt—with smartboards or 1:1 devices or makerspaces or whatever the next innovation-of-the-day might be—are doomed to become obsolete and leave the students they serve behind.

The counterpoint to this optimistic narrative is what we might call the *techno-pessimist* narrative. In this view, technology looms as a corrosive threat to organic human and natural relations. This isn't a new idea; 19th-century Romantic poets like William Blake mourned the incursion of industrial technologies and "dark satanic mills" that blighted the pastoral scenery of their country landscapes. Like these writers, today's techno-pessimists similarly worry that something pure and authentic is being lost in the spread of technology. Bestselling books caution that mobile devices and social media offer only superficial connection, which is incrementally inhibiting our ability to form real human bonds and to participate in meaningful face-to-face dialogue (Turkle, 2017). Widely shared op-eds, likewise, warn that digital technologies are impairing our ability to read (Wolf, 2018) and reason (Carr, 2008), all while making us feel less happy and less fulfilled (Twenge, 2017). These techno-pessimists advocate for more restrained and disciplined usage of technology, and for more forms of non-digital inter-action in everyday life. Such views have informed school and classroom practices in various ways, from imposing limits on students' screen time to imparting lessons on "digital citizenship" that emphasize the need for moderating online activities. Some elite independent schools, including those (ironically enough) that Bill Gates's and Steve Jobs's children attended, now even advertise "tech-free" environments where students can learn and inter-act without the distractions of networked devices and screens (Weller, 2017; cf. Ames, 2019).

On the surface, these techno-optimist and techno-pessimist narratives couldn't be more different, but they actually have more in common than initially meets the eye. If we look closely, we can see that these celebrations of, and anxieties about, technology each share a linear view of technological innovation. The techno-optimist sees new developments as part of a long arc bending toward progress, the techno-pessimist sees them as a steady retreat from venerable norms and practices once unsullied by digital media-tion. These views are two sides of the same coin. Each positions technology as an engine of inevitable transformation; they only differ in whether they understand this transformation to be positive or negative.

The term that scholars use for this linear view is *technological deter-minism* (Smith & Marx, 1994). As the name suggests, this is the belief that technologies determine social outcomes by bringing about preordained consequences—be they good or bad. It's a widely held perspective partly because it makes intuitive sense. On the optimistic side, it's easy to look at the stream of inventions that have raised our standard of living over the last two centuries—railroads, electricity, cars, refrigeration, air travel, comput-ers, the Internet, mobile phones—and conclude that even better creations must be on the horizon. On the pessimistic side, it's equally easy to look at the negative impacts of these innovations—natural resource extraction, pol-lution, labor exploitation, social fragmentation, rampant disinformation—and see the world in a state of technology-induced decay.

What each of these techno-determinist positions miss is that there is nothing inevitable about technological development or its consequences. While it is true that some of the most dramatic medical and industrial achievements in human history occurred over the last 200 years, there is no reason to expect things to continue at this same volume or pace into the future. Indeed, economic historian Robert Gordon (2016) argues that most "new" inventions from the last 50 years are primarily adaptations and optimizations of technologies that existed in some form by 1970. In this view, it could be said that we are currently living in a period not of inventive advancement, but stagnation, or even decline.

Further, different communities and individuals experience the impacts of technologies differently, which prevents them from being slotted into simple characterizations as "good" or "bad." Pessimists are right to point out that technologies can be detrimental to humans and nature. Advances in Western medicine, for instance, have come at the expense of marginalized and colonized communities, which were often forced into deadly experiments and procedures in the name of scientific progress (Anderson, 2006; Washington, 2008). Likewise, there is no doubt that the ongoing destruction of the planet has accelerated under the conditions of advanced industrialization (Chakrabarty, 2009). Technological progress, in other words, should not be confused with moral or political progress. But optimists, too, are right to point out that anxieties about technology are often rooted in a nostalgic attachment to norms and ideals that might well be worth questioning. Just over a century ago Victorians were frightened that the popularity of bicycles—a then-emerging technology—would soon erode the physical, mental, and moral health of English society (particularly women) (Strange & Brown, 2002). It is likely that some of today's techno-pessimistic panics will sound as silly to folks in the future as these do to us today.

Common as it is, technological determinism doesn't offer a satisfactory approach for thinking about technology and its impacts. Deep down, we already know this from experience. If you're like me, you probably don't see yourself fitting neatly into either the optimistic or pessimistic camps. That's because most people hold some version of these contradictory positions in their head at the same time. We're optimists about the technologies that make life easier or better, and we're pessimists about those that don't. When our students are texting or browsing social media during class, it's a sign of technology-induced distractedness and inattention. When we do the same thing in a faculty meeting, it's a form of multitasking. This is another way of saying that celebrations of technology and anxieties about technology don't inhere in the devices themselves, but in their situated meanings and uses in our lives and the lives of others. For this reason, another orientation toward technology is needed—one that resists grand, deterministic pronouncements and instead attends to the relations between technologies and everyday situations. We can call these relations "technological infrastructures."

TECHNOLOGY AS INFRASTRUCTURE

Technological infrastructures are both similar to and different from the other kinds of infrastructure we've explored so far. They are similar in the sense that they refer to the underlying (even hidden) mechanisms that condition observable practices in schools. Just as different imaginative infrastructures can inject contradictory interests into classrooms, and conflicting pedagogical infrastructures can undermine the best laid plans of educators, technological infrastructures can support or obstruct teaching and learning, depending on how they are configured. Jade's phone, for instance, allowed her to engage in forms of creative expression (through her Notes and video production apps), but it also limited how her creative work could be shared (through the latter app's export features). As we will see, this incongruity arises from the infrastructural arrangements that linked her phone and its software to the situated setting of her classroom.

However, technological infrastructures are also different in an important way: their *scale*. The mechanisms that allow technologies to operate are often far more expansive than we first realize. Consider the automobile. What infrastructures are involved in using a car? For starters, there's the infrastructure of laws and norms that allow motorists to navigate roads safely. This is likely the infrastructure that people are most conscious of when they are driving. But we can also zoom in on the underlying infrastructure of the automotive technology itself: the design of the body, engine, and brakes. Most drivers don't think much about this infrastructure hidden beneath the hood until it malfunctions, but it's foundational if one wants to use a car to get around.

To press our example further, we might also zoom out to the infrastructures of fuel and roadways. Cars are only useable to the extent that they have energy to make them run and can drive on roads that connect drivers from where they are to where they want to go. In the United States, much of the last century was devoted to making these infrastructures available to drivers; over 4 million miles of road were carved into the landscape, cities and suburbs were re-structured around commuter routes, natural ecosystems were ravaged, global industries were birthed, and transnational trade agreements were forged. In other words, while using a car might feel like an individual or localized activity, it relies on infrastructures that link it to historical and present-day processes at vastly different scales. Of course, we probably aren't contemplating the inner workings of internal combustion engines or the nuances of global energy policy each time we get into a car, but they remain critical supports that allow automotive technologies to operate. We can't really say we understand the properties and effects of cars as a technology without grappling with their infrastructural dimensions.

Complicated as this might sound, our automobile example spotlights three categories of technological infrastructure that can help us to think about the situated meanings and uses of technology in schools. My colleague Antero Garcia and I have termed these *social uses, design decisions,* and *material resources* (Garcia & Nichols, 2021). Let's take a closer look at each before we explore how they impacted instruction and learning in the Innovation School.

Social Uses

As the name suggests, this type of infrastructure refers to the ways a technology is used in social settings. This is the dimension of technology to which people are most often attuned. In our automobile example, this would include both the laws associated with safe driving (i.e., the "intended use" of cars) as well as the practices of real, everyday motorists (i.e., their "actual use"). In my work with teachers and administrators, the most common questions I hear about technology are related to social uses. When educators ask about technology recommendations ("What's a good app for teaching algebra?"), they're hoping to find a tool that aligns with some intended usage they have in mind. When they ask about how to manage devices ("How do I keep students from texting in class?"), they are looking to monitor or control the actual use of technology in the classroom.

The gap between the intended and actual uses of technology is hard to avoid. Students, classrooms, and schools are unpredictable. So there's no way to perfectly anticipate how a technology will alter teaching, learning, and interactions in a given setting. Early in the COVID-19 pandemic, for instance, many educators turned to services like Zoom and Google Meet—platforms whose intended use promised to replicate in-person instruction. However, a number of unexpected variables (e.g., technical difficulties, a lack of in-home privacy, and students' reluctance to turn on video cameras) quickly impacted the actual use of these apps. It is because of this unpredictability that social uses need to be understood not as fixed or predetermined outcomes that unfold once a technology is implemented, but as an outgrowth of intended and actual usage bumping against one another. How these different uses converge, then, is an infrastructure that shapes the impacts a technology will have in practice.

Design Decisions

The second type of infrastructure relates to the design of a technology. Technologies are not born into the world fully formed. Like any innovation, each represents the accumulation of thousands of human decisions about how it will look, what it will do, and how it will function. In our automobile example, decisions related to the structure of a car body, the inner workings of its engine, and the aesthetics of its interior fit into this category. Even though users are often far removed from these choices, they are impacted by them in subtle and overt ways. The design decision to include seatbelts in cars in the 1960s, for instance, has had a dramatic effect on the social uses and outcomes of automobiles over the last half century.

Design decisions play an especially important role in the digital technologies that have become commonplace in education. Every app, software service, or platform introduced into a school or classroom setting carries the choices (and, by extension, the values and interests) of its programmers, engineers, graphic designers, marketers, and business advisors. These choices influence important aspects of how the technology works, including its:

- *Interface*—the visual layout and usability of the app or platform
- *Data management*—what information the software will collect about its users and usage (and how that data will be used and stored)
- *Algorithms*—the formulas that translate users' data into personalized content
- *Governance*—how activities are monitored or regulated on the app or platform
- *Ownership*—whose property the app or platform, and the data generated from it, are
- *Business model*—how the app or platform makes money

Like in our car example, even though many of these decisions are hidden from everyday users, they have important implications for schools and classrooms. Sometimes these implications are logistical. A clunky interface, for example, may mean that students will need more time or support to use certain software. A change in a platform's business model may hide once-accessible features behind a paywall, leaving teachers to seek out free or inexpensive alternatives as beloved and dependable resources become unusable (Nichols & LeBlanc, 2020).

Other times, the implications of design decisions can be more severe. Because design decisions are made by humans, digital technologies often end up reflecting the personalities and priorities of their creators. Scholars like Safiya Noble (2018), Ruha Benjamin (2019), and Virginia Eubanks (2018) have demonstrated that technologies often inherit biases from their designers, and that these biases have a disproportionately negative effect on people from racially and economically marginalized communities. For example, Zoom—the video conferencing platform that played a significant role in facilitating online learning during the COVID-19 pandemic—uses algorithms to detect faces and generate virtual backgrounds. These algorithms have been shown to be less accurate for non-White users (Dickey, 2020), making such features more difficult for students and teachers of color to use without seeing their faces disappear. In my own collaborative research, we have found similar exclusionary outcomes from the use of "personalized" learning apps in classrooms (Dixon-Román et al., 2020; Nichols et al., 2021). For instance, adaptive technologies for assessing and giving individualized feedback on students' writing often fail to recognize language varieties—regional dialects, African American English, and translanguaging—and proceed to categorize them as wrong or in need of revision. The software's algorithmic design, a process commonly referred to as "natural language processing," thus gives shape to which kinds of writing and language in schools are deemed acceptable or *un*natural.

Ruha Benjamin (2019) uses the term *discriminatory design* to describe such instances, where the behind-the-scenes decisions of designers have powerful downstream implications not only for how technologies are used, but for how inequities are reproduced. Implicit in this term is its opposite—the possibility that different choices might lead to inclusive and liberatory outcomes—which Sasha Costanza-Chock (2020) calls *design justice*. Attending to design decisions as a technological infrastructure is crucial not only for rooting out bias and discrimination, but also for considering how technologies might better align with the interests and commitments of educators and students.

Material Resources

The third type of infrastructure involves the material resources needed to implement and sustain the use of a technology. Like design decisions, these infrastructures can be easy to overlook because they are often far removed from the everyday experience of people who use them. Recall from our automobile example: Most drivers don't think much about the trade agreements, pipelines, and environmental extractions that keep their fuel tanks filled. Yet their vehicles would not be operable without these infrastructures. But it's not just distance from users' experience that causes material resources to get overlooked, it's their *nearness* as well. Roadways, we have seen, are foundational infrastructures for cars to operate, but they are so ubiquitous, it is easy to forget that they haven't always been there. Just as a fish might strain to see the water around it, it's easy for us to look past the material supports we are most dependent on.

Digital technologies can be particularly invisible because they have an immaterial quality to them. There is an airy, even disembodied, way that we talk about connective media as "wireless" devices that store files in "the cloud." Even our casual distinctions between things occurring in virtual spaces and "in real life" (or "IRL," as the kids once said) make digital media seem ephemeral. But the truth is that all of these activities rely on material infrastructures. Even though when we send a text message, it seems to just appear on someone else's phone, this is only possible due to vast networks of undersea cables, electrical grids, telecom wiring, and energy-guzzling server farms—not to mention the rare minerals and physical labor that went into producing our computers, phones, and routers. It takes a lot of material resources, working in harmony, to make digital technologies feel immaterial.

For many educators, the materiality of digital media became all too apparent during the COVID-19 pandemic. Frustrations with unstable Internet connections, malfunctioning microphones, and sluggish hardware revealed certain material infrastructures that we took for granted. The pandemic laid bare the ways that necessary material resources are not equally accessible or usable for everyone. Even in schools with 1:1 devices, a spotty Wi-Fi connection can bring online class assignments to a standstill or create obstacles for students completing assignments from home. Looking at these material resources as a kind of infrastructure allows educators to consider how the technologies they use tether schools and classrooms to certain instructional practices, spending priorities, and consumption habits. The ripple effects of these dependencies have implications for the equity of students and communities.

Missing the Tree for the Leaves

If you've made it this far into this book, it will not surprise you to hear that these three types of technological infrastructure are interrelated. As with other infrastructures we've explored, changes in one category often have ripple effects on others. The observable, social uses of a technology are inseparable from the design decisions that underwrite that product or service and the material resources that are necessary for it to operate.

A helpful way to think about these relations, which I've adapted from the media theorist José van Dijck (2020), is to visualize them as a tree (Figure 3.1; cf. Garcia & Nichols, 2021). The various tools and devices that we use each day, and the practices associated with them (i.e., the social uses) are the tree's leaves. They may appear to be complete unto themselves, but they're best understood as part of a larger organism. That organism includes the trunk (which gives it structure, much like design decisions do) and the roots (which gives it nutrients and energy—material resources). When we focus only on implementing and using specific tools and apps in schools, we can easily miss the tree for the leaves. It's like using a Kindle reader or

Figure 3.1. Visualizing relations among three types of technological infrastructures.

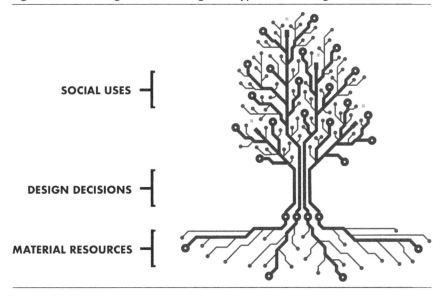

streaming films from Prime Video without considering their relationship to Amazon, or thinking about that corporation's influence on the economy, the environment, and popular culture. Of course, we can choose *not* to think about these things, but when we do, we miss an opportunity to better understand the technology we're using and how it affects teaching, learning, and the wider world around us.

Ignoring these supporting dimensions also prevents us from seeing how technological infrastructures work with or against the other types of infrastructure we've discussed so far in this book. For instance, the social usage of a classroom management app may align nicely with certain pedagogical infrastructures (Chapter 2) for school administration. However, if the design decisions behind that app are structured to harvest salable data from students, this may undermine the interests and aims of an educator whose imaginative infrastructure (Chapter 1) for innovation is rooted in social justice. Similarly, we can see in Jade's story from earlier in the chapter how the social use of her video production app aligned with certain pedagogical infrastructures but not others. The design decisions behind the app were effective as communicative supports as she created her project, but they were incompatible with the administrative supports that the teacher used to assess and respond to student work. In this way, thinking about technological infrastructures can orient educators to ask deeper questions about the competing imperatives that technologies introduce into schools, and the impacts these have for teaching and learning (see Table 3.1). In turn, these impacts can drive more intentional decision-making when it comes to implementing, using, resisting, or avoiding certain technologies in schools.

Glitches

As we've seen in previous chapters, one of the primary ways that we can recognize infrastructural alignments and disconnects is by looking closely at moments of breakdown that arise in practice. My colleague Bethany Monea and I (Nichols & Monea, 2019) refer to the frictions within and between technological infrastructures by the familiar name *glitches*. In everyday usage, the term "glitch" usually signals some kind of issue or instability related to technology. Most educators have experienced the frustration of a glitch in their practice—a copy machine jam, a computer that refused to project a presentation, an unresponsive app, or a spotty Wi-Fi connection.

People tend think of such glitches as momentary malfunctions. Sometimes that is the case; I've certainly "repaired" my share of technologies by turning them off and then turning them on again. However, sometimes glitches aren't standalone problems, but the result of larger systemic issues. A printer jam or bad wireless connection can be brief breakdowns, but they might also be an outgrowth of wider policy and funding choices that have left schools using nonoperational technologies beyond their lifespan, or made certain

Table 3.1. Educator questions for exploring technological infrastructures.

Technological Infrastructure	Questions for educators
Social uses	• How will this technology shape learning and interaction in my classroom or school? • In what ways might this reshaping align with, or work against already existing supports and practices (i.e., pedagogical infrastructures)? • In what ways might this reshaping align with (or diverge from) my interests and commitments as an educator (i.e., imaginative infrastructures)?
Design decisions	• What users did the designers have in mind when creating this technology? How are these potential users similar to or different from my students? • What barriers might the design of these technologies create for students? • Do complicated technical requirements prohibit some students from meaningful engagement with this technology? • What larger entities and interests does this technology connect my classroom to (e.g., data harvesting, corporate growth, third-party influence over public education)? • How do the answers to such questions line up with my own (and my students') imaginative infrastructures for the classroom? With my already existing pedagogical infrastructures?
Material resources	• What changes will I need to make in my classroom design and structure to use this technology? • What material infrastructures does this technology tether my classroom or school to (i.e., dependable Wi-Fi, charged devices, subscription costs and software updates)? • How do these dependencies align with or work against my imaginative infrastructures for the classroom? With my already existing pedagogical infrastructures?

neighborhoods less equipped for reliable high-speed Internet access. In other words, "glitches" often have a bigger story to tell than we might initially expect. Treating them not as anomalies, but as indicators of where, how, and for whom our technological infrastructures are working (or not working) helps identify the situated role technologies play in schools. Even more, they can point to possibilities for proactively confronting and intervening in places where these infrastructures are not serving the interests of educators, students, and communities.

In what follows, we'll explore how glitches can attune us to how technological infrastructures operate in classrooms by taking a close look at a case from the Innovation School's Media Makerspace. The case involves three students—Kyrie, Kendrick, and Dante—who were tasked with creating a collaborative "digital story," a creative genre that combines spoken word, text, music, and video into a short digital film (Hull, 2003). I've selected this case not because of how striking or pronounced the glitches the students encountered were, but because of their subtlety. In fact, the teachers and the research team didn't notice these glitches at all at the time— much less recognize them as breakdowns in the classroom's technological infrastructure. In the moment, we saw Kyrie, Kendrick, and Dante's project as an exemplary testament to the power of students using technology for creative expression and social critique. It was not until months later, in an end-of-year interview with Kendrick, that we learned how frustrating the project had been for the group. "We couldn't make it like we wanted to," he said. This prompted me to return to field notes, recordings, and other project data to understand what had gone awry, and to consider how educators might identify and respond to such glitches when they arise in classrooms.

"WHERE WE'RE FROM": GLITCHES IN STUDENTS' DIGITAL STORYTELLING

Our case begins in the Media Makerspace during the Innovation School's first year. Students had recently completed a unit in their humanities classes about identity, in which they had written "Where I'm From" poems, modeled on George Ella Lyon's text of the same name. In her poem, Lyon lists people, objects, and snippets of dialogue from her youth—suggesting, to readers, that she is "from" these memories, as they have shaped the person she is today. Using this template, the students produced powerful poems about the places, artifacts, and communities that made them who they are. Their work was so moving in fact, that Sam—a humanities teacher and Lab Leader for the school's makerspaces—had the idea of extending the project into the Media Makerspace. For this project, students would work in groups to remix their individual "Where I'm From" poems into a collaborative "Where We're From" digital story, making use of the cameras, audio recorders, and video editing equipment available in the makerspace. To support the students, Sam provided them resources for storyboarding their projects, as well as video-editing tutorials with the iMovie software on the makerspace computers.

From the moment Sam introduced the project, Kyrie, Kendrick, and Dante were energized. Like other students, they had taken the "Where I'm From" poetry assignment seriously, reflecting on how they had been influenced by their city, neighborhood, and families. Kendrick wrote about his complicated relationship with his father; Kyrie wrote about his activism and advocacy against gun violence; and Dante celebrated the historical figures— such as Martin Luther King, Jr., and James Baldwin—whose words and actions moved him to fight for racial justice. The three were close friends who had great respect for one another's stories and abilities. They were excited for the opportunity to braid elements from their independent work into a collective composition. Over the course of the project, however, their social usage of technology to create their digital story bumped up against design decisions and material constraints that were not immediately visible to them, Sam, or the research team members. Even as the students persisted, creatively collaborating to work around such obstacles, three glitches tempered their enthusiasm for the project they produced.

Glitch #1: Search Algorithms

The first glitch surfaced early in the group's collaboration. After the trio formed, they sat at a table and laid out their individual "Where I'm From" poems to read through them together. As they did, each offered suggestions for which individual lines ought to be integrated into the collaborative remix, and how they might be altered or amended so they could flow as a cohesive whole. Kyrie and Dante suggested that Kendrick, a talented rapper, take a first pass smoothing out a synthesized draft that incorporated their disparate ideas. Kendrick jumped at the opportunity to mold the group's lines into a composition with a meter and cadence that matched the force of a spoken word poem or rap verse. Almost immediately, he took the group's notes to a corner of the room where he bobbed his head and mouthed words to an imagined beat, pausing periodically to scribble down another line. The following day, he returned to class with a completed draft (Figure 3.2), telling his group members, "I stayed up all night making it perfect."

After some collective revisions and adjustments to Kendrick's text, the group began storyboarding visuals to accompany their remix. It was while trying to find these images that the first (and most insidious) glitch occurred. Originally, the group had planned to open their digital story with an image of the city skyline, followed by a picture from their neighborhood taken just a few blocks from the school. They had no trouble locating the first in Google Images, but the second proved more difficult. Searching for "Philadelphia neighborhood" yielded photos of affluent homes and tourist destinations in town—visuals different from what the group wanted to represent. After scrolling for some time, they eventually decided to abandon the depiction from their storyboard, resorting instead to a collage of tourist landmarks that showed up early in the search results.

It would be easy to overlook this glitch: Unsuccessful Google searches are enough of an everyday occurrence that they might not seem to merit much attention. But if we take this momentary malfunction seriously, we can recognize a deeper infrastructural outcome. Kendrick, Kyrie, and Dante's social use of technology (to find images for a creative project) were being shaped by design decisions embedded in Google. In this case, the algorithms

Figure 3.2. Kendrick, Dante, and Kyrie's collaborative poem.

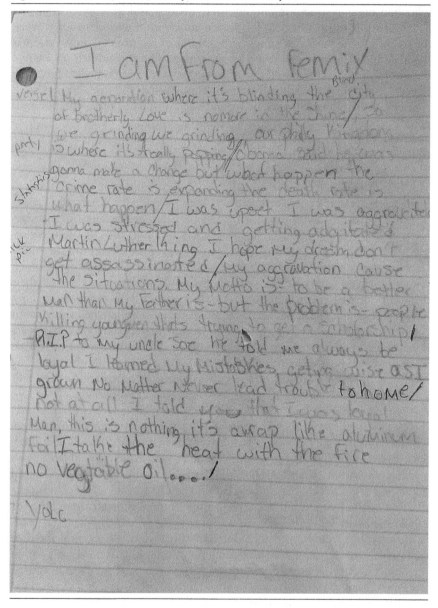

prioritized depictions of certain Philadelphia neighborhoods over others. This is what media scholars refer to as "algorithmic bias." In *Algorithms of Oppression: How Search Engines Reinforce Racism* (2018), Safiya Noble describes how search engines like Google reproduce formations of difference by delivering results under a cloak of algorithmic objectivity that cater to White, straight, cisgender, able-bodied men. For Kyrie, Kendrick, and Dante, this meant that even though their social uses of technology afforded them access to images for their creative work, this access was conditioned by the interests and priorities of distant designers. Ultimately, this incongruity reshaped their composing process, pressuring them to abandon the planned vision for their digital story's opening. Instead, they infused it with imagery reflective of the dominant Internet users to which Google's algorithm was tailored.

It is worth noting that this group was not alone in experiencing this glitch. In returning to field notes after the fact, my colleague Kelly Johnston and I found several references to groups that similarly struggled to locate representative images (cf. Nichols & Johnston, 2020). One group, searching for a photo of a family, almost selected an early Google result—a White couple with two White children—until a research team member suggested that they could amend their search to "Black family" if they wanted alternate images. It is telling that such occasions were striking enough for research team members to record in field notes, yet they were not recognized as a wider pattern until we returned later, looking for such glitches. As I will suggest, this points to the need for technological infrastructures to be foregrounded in teaching and learning, so that glitches can be understood not as anomalies, but as everyday occurrences that demand pedagogical attention.

Glitch #2: Governance and Business Models

While Kendrick was off in a corner working on his poem remix for the first day of the project, Kyrie and Dante were busy looking for music that could accompany their digital story. Phones in hand, they took turns playing clips from different songs, discussing which tones and rhythms would best match their composition. After some time, they found a perfect match. Dante played a local rapper's track, which broke up its verses with audio from several authentic city news reports. Kyrie liked the idea of syncing the track so that these news clippings would punctuate their poem with actual reporting from their town. They played the song for Kendrick, who was equally enthusiastic.

However, importing the song into the project surfaced a second glitch. Dante had access to the song using a subscription-based music service, but there was no way for him to download it onto the iMac where they were assembling their project. After some troubleshooting, he and Kyrie devised a workaround. They located the song on YouTube and attempted to download it using a YouTube-to-MP3 converter. But the school's firewall blocked this site—as it did the pirating website they tried next. Frustrated, Kyrie decided it was a lost cause and offered to create a backing track using online beat-making software. It was better than iMovie's prepackaged soundtracks, but even so, it was disappointing—they'd found the perfect song for their project, and once again they found themselves settling for a second-rate alternative.

This glitch, very different from the first, surfaced as design decisions related to governance and business models that mediated the group's access to materials. Governance is reflected in the constraints that made the group's preferred song available, just not in a form usable in their digital story—an incompatibility between Dante's music subscription and iMovie's importing capabilities. Such breakdowns may appear as unfortunate software flaws, but they only exist because humans have designed them to operate this way. Behind any technology are human choices about what problems should be solved (or not), and which practices should be possible (or prohibited). Technologies are always embedded with the interests, aims, and values of those who created it. Which is to say, technologies are always political.

This is true not only of iMovie—which is owned by Apple, a company with an interest in controlling how music is circulated and used—but also of the school's firewall, which regulates the resources available to students as they create, improvise, and troubleshoot projects. In both instances, the governance structures of the software were closely tied to a business model that enjoined the music industry and digital streaming services, and that adjudicated proper from improper ways of accessing and using commercial content. This is not to suggest that such regulation is necessarily bad—only that it is unavoidably present in the social uses of technology in schools.

For Dante, Kyrie, and Kendrick, this glitch meant that their vision for the project was intimately entangled with the constraints of intellectual property law and corporate profit motives. As scholars of media law have argued, these regulations are rarely designed to support (much less endorse) the forms of creative remixing that connective media might otherwise make available (Lessig, 2008). Even as Kyrie's homemade track reflects the group's ingenuity in working within and against the constraints of the glitches they encountered, their workaround demonstrates the force that technological infrastructures can play in shaping the usage of technology in classrooms.

Glitch #3: Software Interfaces

With images and music inserted into iMovie, all that remained was for Kendrick to record the vocals of their remix, and for Kyrie and Dante to smooth out timing and transitions in the video. Pacing around the computer, Kendrick rehearsed his delivery, mouthing the words to find the right rhythm before recording. For his first take, Kendrick rapped the entire poem, only to find that he was out of sync with the background music. He tried a second time, allowing the beat to play softly so that he could monitor his own timing. But now, the mic picked up the snare of the soft backing beat, creating an odd syncopation. After more takes—now with headphones on to mute the background noise—Kyrie suggested recording one section at a time, producing audio that they could splice together afterward in iMovie.

Editing these segments surfaced a third glitch. Although Kyrie, an aspiring music producer, had experience using audio engineering software, he struggled to align audio segments in iMovie's clunky interface. For several days, the group tinkered with the audio, trying to get it perfectly matched to the beat and images. They even stayed in the makerspace during lunch to re-record vocals for a particularly complex section of the remix. But as the software continued to give them problems, frustration set in. They began deleting some of the more technically complicated lines from the poem, hoping to make it possible to sync. In the end, they never managed to align the audio as they planned. When they presented the project to their classmates, Kendrick opted to rap the poem live while the music, images, and text from the digital story projected behind him. This was, once again, a creative workaround that demonstrates their commitment to the project, but it was also a significant departure from their planned vision. The lack of a polished video with audio also meant that the project could not be easily shared with friends or family outside of the class.

This glitch emerged from the interplay of two technological infrastructures—material resources (i.e., the software made available to students) and design decisions (i.e., the interface of the software and its narrow capacities for audio editing). Even though iMovie let the students edit, rearrange, and revise their work, it was not a neutral mediator in this process. The software became a clumsy coauthor, molding the group's project to fit its most frustrating limitations. This imposition was clearest in the students' willingness, in a moment of desperation, to cut lines from the poem to make it work with the program. Still, it is easy to overlook the active role that software plays in shaping how it gets used. Design theorist Johanna Drucker (2013) suggests this is because we tend to look *through*, not *at*, the screens and interfaces that mediate our digital activities. In reality, she argues, interfaces like iMovie are not just tools that students use, but a "border zone between cultural systems" (p. 216). In this case, iMovie was where students' aspirations and creative practices bumped up against the material constraints of the school's technology budget and the design choices of iMovie's creators. The glitches that arose in this border zone point back to these infrastructures that young people and their teachers work with, within, and against when these technologies are folded into instruction and learning.

GLITCHES AND (IN)EQUITY IN INNOVATIVE EDUCATION

Reading across the glitches that surfaced in Kendrick, Kyrie, and Dante's project helps reveal the presence and work of technological infrastructures in their—and in most—innovative classrooms. In doing so, it also complicates several well-rehearsed stories frequently told about technology, teaching, and learning. The most immediate of these stories is that of technological determinism. It would be difficult to look at the group's process of creating their digital story and to conclude that "technology" functioned in any singular, linear, or universal way. A techno-optimist could argue that, despite some setbacks, the students' project was more engaging, collaborative, and demanding because of the technologies used. Technology brought it a pedagogical step forward. A techno-pessimist could just as easily spotlight the setbacks (e.g., algorithmic bias, proprietary content, clunky interfaces) as corrosive effects of technology that undo whatever positive features the project offered. In truth, neither position is right or wrong. Technology always gives and takes, even in the same project. We can see it in Kendrick, Kyrie, and Dante's initial excitement for—and eventual disappointment with—their digital story, just as we saw it in the creative breakthroughs and breakdowns that Jade encountered when she used her phone for poetic and film compositions. This is why deterministic perspectives can only get us so far; they are so fixated on tallying the costs or benefits of a technology that they miss the more urgent need to understand the situated ways that technologies function, the real work they do in the world, and the downstream impacts that result from their use. They are so concerned, in other words, with whether a technology is "good" or "bad" that they forget to ask: Good or bad for whom? For what purposes, and under what circumstances?

One example of how determinism creeps into pedagogy—and another common story that our case study complicates—is the idea of the "digital native." This term, coined and popularized by education consultant Marc Prensky (2010), reflects the widespread belief that young people have an innate connection to technology that sets them apart from their elders, who are merely "digital immigrants." It isn't a new idea; 30 years ago, computer science experts saw potential for PCs to be "children's machines"—tools for thinking and creative expression that young people would recognize as uniquely *theirs* (Papert, 1993, p. ix). But over time, this sense of possibility has been conflated with one of inevitability—resulting in popular, if misleading, truisms about the powerful, even mystical, bonds that young people share with computer technologies.

There are a few reasons people gravitate to such truisms. For one, it offers up "digital technology" as a convenient explanation for the differences between generations. An unending parade of books has centered technology as a key to understanding and classifying millennials, GenZers, and even successive generations: *the Google generation* (Gunter et al., 2009), *the app generation* (Gardner & Davis, 2014), *the connected generation* (Hayman & Coleman, 2016), *the iGeneration* (Twenge, 2018), *the tech generation* (Brooks & Lasser, 2018), and *the distracted generation* (Wigley, 2021), to name a few. Categorizations like these are popular partly because they are comforting. They allow people to confidently abdicate responsibility to technology for the virtues (on the optimistic side) or deficits (on the pessimistic side) they perceive in younger generations. Avoidance is always more soothing than confronting the reality that the effects of technology are uneven and unpredictable for everyone. Kendrick, Kyrie, and Dante's project demonstrates how fluency with technology can allow students to persevere through creative workarounds and multiple obstacles. It also shows that their fluency does not operate independently from the situated setting of the classroom and the technological infrastructures they must contend with. The "digital native" myth is an expedient way to paper over these complexities, reducing the question of technology to a matter of addition or subtraction—that is, adding more technologies so that "digital natives" can thrive, or removing them so that "the distracted generation" can focus more intently on their lessons. But access to (or removal of) technology does not alone lead to equitable or joyful learning.

Another reason for the persistence of this digital native myth is that it accords with the common conception that youth are inherently empowered when they have opportunities to create or compose in non-print formats at school, such as by making websites, creating videos, and recording podcasts. This idea stems from the myth's emergence in the 1990s and 2000s alongside the general optimism surrounding the advent of Web 2.0 technologies. At the time, there was a widespread sense that the Internet was creating a new public sphere where anyone, regardless of background, could freely converse, connect, and collaborate with others (Benkler, 2007). Young people played an important role in such conceptualizations, as it was digital natives who were helping to shape the "democratic ethos" and "participatory culture" that were associated with early social networks, like YouTube and MySpace (Jenkins, 2006). Educators, in turn, advocated for integrating such practices into classrooms—for instance, by adding "new literacies" or "21st-century skills" related to peer-production to the curriculum (Lankshear & Knobel, 2011), or incorporating students' social media practices into everyday assignments (Lewis, 2010). Doing so, it was suggested, would not only help keep schools innovative and relevant, it would also empower students by affirming their out-of-school interests in the formal classroom.

Of course, the last decade has complicated these rosy projections. The "public" sphere of the Internet, if it ever existed, was quickly consolidated in the hands of a few private corporations like Google and Facebook. Even more disturbing, Edward Snowden's 2013 NSA leaks revealed that these corporations had also been aiding the U.S. government in massive domestic and international surveillance campaigns. It also turned out that the same connectivity that allowed social networks to facilitate generative forms of sharing and collaboration could just as easily be used for more nefarious purposes—like bolstering misinformation, voter suppression, and white nationalism. In other words, the democratic ethos ascribed to the Internet was not endemic to the technology itself. Rather, this was one of the many potential uses of the technology. In the context of education, this means that, while the impulse to make room for students' out-of-school interests and technological abilities in the classroom was (and has always been) correct, the assumption that this would lead inevitably toward empowerment was not. As Kendrick, Kyrie, and Dante's project shows, access to technology and interest-driven assignments do not solely lead to empowering outcomes for students. It is only by paying attention to the infrastructures that animate such activities that we can begin to understand the competing pressures that young people work with and against when they produce media artifacts in schools.

Crucially, this focus on technological infrastructures can also re-attune us to the relationship between technologies and educational equity. While deterministic narratives about the liberatory effects of closing "technology gaps" in schools or putting new innovations in the hands of "digital natives" may claim to serve equitable ends, in practice they often work against them. Such approaches center technology as an agent of change and assume that access to technology is the biggest obstacle to be overcome in ensuring just and inclusive learning. As we have seen, this is not the case. The glitches that Kendrick, Kyrie, and Dante encountered did not stem from a lack of access to technology, but from the underlying infrastructures that animated their technology-driven activities and the interoperation of these infrastructures with the classroom setting of the Innovation School. A focus on access alone doesn't only overlook such glitches, it also neglects the uneven ways that glitches surface in schools (cf. Litts et al., 2021). For instance, the second and third glitches the group faced could have occurred in any classroom where students were searching for music or struggling to use a particular software application. However, the first specifically impacts students whose racial, sexual, gender, and class identities diverge from the dominant norms of White heteropatriarchy embedded in Google's search algorithm. An infrastructural perspective can direct educators' attention to alleviate such inequities in ways that deterministic approaches cannot.

An infrastructural orientation toward technology also has pedagogical implications. Deterministic views tend to encourage educators to teach with, rather than about, technology. They are told to assign it for classes to use, rather than to investigate it alongside their students. That is, a deterministic view absolves educators of the responsibility to think about how technological tools shape what gets said, done, taught, or learned in their schools. One of the troubling consequences of this is that when glitches arise and technologies malfunction, it becomes easy for students to see these frictions as personal failures rather than effects of the technological infrastructures at work in the classroom. Kendrick, Kyrie, and Dante's project is an example of this.

Both Sam and the research team were focused on the powerful ways that the students had used technology as a means of creative and collaborative expression. This made it difficult to recognize the glitches the group was working against, and how they impacted the students' experience of the project. I initially saw the group's presentation as a success; it was not until months later that I learned just how disappointing it was for them. In his year-end interview, Kendrick identified the project as a low point in the year because of the mismatch between what he had wanted the project to be and what it ended up being. Without a framework for recognizing the active role technologies played in producing this mismatch, Kendrick placed the blame for the project's failure on himself.

The ease with which systemic technology issues can be conflated with personal shortcomings suggests the importance of centering glitches in teaching and learning. They are not aberrations, but a normal part of existence in a world increasingly mediated by technologies, both digital and analog. As such, they offer a powerful opportunity for instruction and inquiry by drawing attention to the social uses, design decisions, and material resources that animate such devices. Importantly, they also allow us to go even further—not just identifying and evaluating the glitches that arise from practice, but also considering what agentive steps might be possible to intervene in the infrastructures that produce them. Glitches need not only be things that happen to us; we can also use them as entry points for creative and critical action with and against technology (cf. Kafai et al., 2021). By attending to the underlying infrastructures of our devices, we are better equipped to subvert, hack, or creatively misuse technologies so as to bend their infrastructures into closer alignment with our own interests, values, and instructional practices as educators. Such an orientation is central to the shift of seeing "innovation from below" as a framework not just for analyzing already-existing innovations, but for building new ones. It is to this shift that we turn in the next chapter.

CHAPTER 4

Innovating From Below

It's nearing the end of the Innovation School's fourth year. In just a few weeks, students from its inaugural cohort will walk across the auditorium stage and receive their diplomas. Even though my official role as project manager of the university–school partnership ended last year, I've returned to spend a few days with the teachers and students I worked with and learned from since the school opened. They built and molded the Innovation School into what it was today.

In many ways, it is a very different school than it was when we began. Some teachers and students have left, and others have arrived. Classroom practices have been introduced, adapted, and abandoned. Even the school space looks different. Student-created murals and artwork line the once-sparse hallways. Rooms that had been unused and closed off a few years prior due to district budget cuts now had that warm and lived-in feel that came from the accrued energy of 250 teenagers—along with the joys, anxieties, ambitions, and dreams they carried with them.

My return was prompted by another change: the Senior Project Showcase. When the school opened, an emphasis had been placed on "asynchronous" and "personalized" learning. However, as the first graduating class entered its final year, the teachers realized that this focus overlooked something important about how individual autonomy works in tandem with collective action. They devised the Senior Project as a capstone that could merge the two. Students would identify a topic of personal or social significance to use as a springboard for creating (1) a research essay, (2) a media artifact (e.g., a film, song, poem, short story, etc.), (3) a community action or organizing project, and (4) a presentation that synthesized this work for a public audience. I was returning because I'd been invited to serve as a respondent for these presentations.

Watching the showcase, I was struck by the deep and powerful learning on display. Students had not only taken on the challenge of studying complex issues that mattered to them—mass incarceration, mental health, wealth inequality, anti-Blackness, and LGBTQ+ discrimination—but they had also leveraged the school's Media and Community Organizing Makerspaces to develop responses and interventions. They spoke passionately and authoritatively about the work they had done in their projects. Even students whom

I'd seen in past years straining to accommodate themselves to the varied district-, school-, and classroom-level forms of "innovative" education at work in the school now seemed to be thriving in this setting.

Talking with several teachers afterward, I mentioned how moved I'd been by the showcase and the growth I'd seen in the student presenters since they'd first joined the school community. I asked the teachers what they credited the success to. Was it something about the design of the assignment, or the supports they'd put in place that helped students flourish? What, I wondered, had separated this project from those that so many students struggled with during the school's first years? Their answer was striking in its simplicity. The Senior Project was different because they had not devised and implemented it as a pre-planned innovation. Instead, it had emerged from observing the practices students were effectively using in the school environment. The innovation of the Senior Project, in other words, wasn't the assignment itself, but the infrastructures in place that helped to support and draw out student successes.

Up to this point, we have focused on the important work of understanding how innovations work in practice. In contrast with the linear model of innovation, we have seen that innovations are not part of some inevitable march of progress. Rather, they are upshots of competing interests and imperatives, with downstream impacts that fall unevenly on those who use them (and those they are used on). We have attended to different forms of infrastructure that underwrite the devices, practices, and strategies that are often framed as "innovative." In Chapter 1, we saw how the varied *imaginative* infrastructures of administrators, teachers, students, and communities give shape to different conceptions of what counts as innovation. In Chapter 2, we looked at the ways diverse *pedagogical* infrastructures associated with innovation can work with or against the interests of teachers and students in classrooms. Finally, in Chapter 3, we explored the *technological* infrastructures that tether instruction and learning to the constraints of material resources and the design decisions of technological developers.

Taken together, these orientations have helped us to see innovation "from below"—paying attention to the mechanisms that shape how innovations work, for whom, and under what circumstances. What we have yet to consider is how we might go a step further. What does it mean to not just *see*, but *do* innovation from an infrastructural perspective? This is not to discount the significance of the ground we have covered so far. Being able to identify and analyze the infrastructures of innovation at work in a district, school, or classroom is crucially important for equitable education. But the point isn't to stop at analysis; it's to channel those efforts toward intervention and action. What would it look like to approach innovation in an entirely different way, not as a solution we implement from above, but a practice we build from the ground up? It's to this question that we turn in this chapter.

The response of the teachers to my inquiry about the Senior Project Showcase offers a glimpse into what such an approach entails. In contrast with many of the ostensibly innovative practices we have seen in previous chapters—and perhaps you have seen in your own school experience—this approach does not begin with a ready-made innovation. Instead, it starts with the practices, problems, and successes that already exist in schools and classrooms. As we will see, such organic innovations are not just effective, but even more importantly, they are aligned with the values and commitments of educators to sustainable and equitable teaching and learning.

INNOVATION FROM ABOVE: THREE PITFALLS OF THE LINEAR MODEL

Before exploring what innovating from below looks like, it will be helpful to set the stage by highlighting three pitfalls this orientation helps to address. All three of these pitfalls stem from the linear model of innovation. We have encountered forms of each in the preceding chapters. Pausing here to explicitly name them will allow us to recognize them not as isolated shortcomings of specific innovations, but part of a larger pattern that is endemic to the way that "innovation" is conceptualized by and integrated into schools. Understanding this pattern positions us to articulate an alternative that rejects the assumptions of the linear model.

Pitfall #1: Innovations Are Ready-Made

The first pitfall is the conception of innovations as *ready-made*. This follows from the idea that innovations emerge from outside of the sites where they are implemented, and arrive in the hands of practitioners as fully formed resources waiting to be used. They move, we are often told, in a straight line from research to practice. On the surface, this idea makes sense. It's true that we tend to learn about new devices, apps, teaching techniques, and leadership strategies as they appear in articles, reports, and other professional resources, or after they have already been tested elsewhere. As such, it doesn't feel like a stretch to assume that innovations move unidirectionally, through a research-to-practice pipeline—from university labs and tech development offices into the everyday activities of our own classrooms.

But if we tug at this idea, it quickly begins to unravel. Research, after all, is not a monolith. Studies conducted by corporate behemoths like Google or Amazon, or think tanks committed to privatizing public education, are motivated by very different interests than a community-based research team focused on issues of racial or economic justice in education. Their research begins with different questions and presuppositions, which lead to different findings, recommendations, and innovations for practice. Research, then, always arrives in classrooms freighted with the assumptions that may align with or work against those of the school, teacher, or students. When we treat new technologies and techniques as ready-made, we paper over the contingencies and the politics of the research and development that went into producing them as taken-for-granted innovations.

We have seen a trend toward ready-made innovations throughout the previous chapters. Most of the innovations that the school leaders and teachers aimed to implement were backed by research. Makerspaces, asynchronous learning, competency-based assessment, 1:1 devices—each of these has a rich research literature to suggest that they hold promise for schools and classrooms. So too do many of the new innovations that are now being introduced into schools around the world—virtual and augmented reality, for instance, or artificial intelligence technologies for adaptive learning. But being backed by "research" or "data" alone is not a guarantee that these innovations are inherently aligned with the values and commitments of a school or classroom. The same makerspace setup that works well in one school could be a flop in another.

By positioning innovations as ready-made resources that trickle down from research and development into practice, the linear model shifts educators' attention away from the situated needs of their students and classrooms and toward the implementation of someone else's idea of a must-have innovation.

Pitfall #2: Innovations Are Conflicting

The second pitfall is related to the first. The problem is not just that innovations that trickle down from research to practice have uneven and unpredictable outcomes in different settings; they also *conflict* with other already-existing innovations at work in those sites. Even though it is common to talk about innovations as singular devices or techniques, they are always embedded alongside other innovations and practices—some of which may be incompatible with a new addition.

I see evidence of this pitfall most overtly when I visit a new school or district that I am working with in research or professional development settings. A teacher or administrator will give me a tour of the school's facilities, pointing out the different innovations they are implementing: a new makerspace, 1:1 initiative, writing workshop program, grading policy, or professional learning approach. There is almost a sense in these lists that innovation is an *additive* process; the more innovations that a school or classroom can layer together, the better it is . . . or at least, the less likely it is that people will think it's fallen behind the times. But as we have seen, innovation isn't additive, it's *ecological*.

Every innovation that is added to a classroom environment doesn't just result in the old environment plus a new innovation. It creates an entirely new environment. In Chapter 2, we saw how small changes in the spatial or curricular configuration of the Innovation School's Humanities program had lasting ripple effects that remade the routines, content, and interactions of the classroom. In Chapter 3, we saw how the introduction of certain technologies can delimit what is possible for students to do, make, and say in an assignment. If we are not attuned to such dynamics, it is easy to miss how the infrastructures involved in implementing one innovation might undermine others. A new grading policy can be a powerful intervention only if the rest of the environment into which it is introduced is aligned with it. If not, then the overt or subtle conflicts that result can not only undermine the new innovation—they can work against students' and teachers' interests in classroom conditions for equitable education.

Pitfall #3: Innovations Are Unsustainable

The third pitfall that follows from the linear model is that it often leads to *unsustainable* innovations. There are two main reasons for this. First, as we have said, the innovations that emerge from the linear model often conflict with other innovations already at work in a school. This frustrates those who are stuck using these competing and contradictory innovations, which usually results in them abandoning one or more of them.

Education historian Jack Schneider (2014) has argued that one of the key reasons that innovative ideas and practices fail to stick is that they lack "occupational realism"—the capacity to be efficiently and effectively integrated into actual practice. In other words, a new technology may look great on paper, but the real test of its longevity is how it holds up in use. When an innovation's infrastructures don't play nicely with the other imaginative, pedagogical, or technological infrastructures in an educator's classroom, then it's reasonable for the educator to move on to other devices, techniques, and strategies that will. This is why innovations from above often have such a high turnover rate (cf. Cuban, 1986). But there is also a second reason such innovations are short-lived.

The instability that arises when innovations flounder isn't just an unfortunate side-effect of the linear model; it's central to it. One of the guiding assumptions of a linear view of innovation is that failure is *desirable*. After all, if we believe that innovation moves along a straight path, then failure is a necessary step toward ushering in the next wave of newer and better innovations. This idea is explicitly repeated in the tech world, where it is taken for granted that "disruption" is an inherent good, upending existing routines and practices to make room for the new. Firms like Facebook even adopt company-wide mottos like "Move Fast and Break Things" to signal the centrality of failure to their vision for growth. In the linear model, unsustainability is a feature, not a bug, of innovation.

While this may be an appropriate (if risky) strategy for private technology companies and their venture capitalist backers, it's a reckless way to organize public institutions responsible for the educational experiences of students. We have seen that the failures that follow in the wake of disruption don't always lead to improved innovations. When schools jump on a trendy new technology, curriculum, or teaching strategy only to have it fail to live up to its promises, it can leave educators and students feeling frustrated and demoralized. By encouraging an orientation toward failure, the linear model allocates time, energy, and resources toward unsustainable innovations premised on the possibility of a big payoff that rarely (if ever) materializes. In the process, it also shifts attention away from more sustainable practices that might better support the aims of equitable education.

INNOVATING FROM BELOW

Over the years that I worked with the teachers, students, and other researchers at the Innovation School, we frequently felt the consequences of these pitfalls. Often the educators and research team members even wondered if we were to blame for the shortcomings of different "innovative" interventions. If innovation moves linearly, after all, then anything that doesn't feel like progress must be user error, not a problem with the innovation itself. Over time, we began to unlearn this impulse, and to recognize that the issue was not with us or with the students. Instead, the problem lay with the ways we were thinking about innovation and how it worked. A different approach to innovation was needed—one that didn't begin from the assumptions of the linear model. Through our unlearning process—and later reflecting on and studying it—an alternate orientation began to take shape: what I have called *innovation from below* (cf. Nichols, 2020, 2021).

Unlike the linear model, innovation from below does not begin with ready-made innovations, or try to paper over their contradictions or instabilities in practice. Instead, it takes classrooms as the starting point for meaningful transformation in schools. Doing so involves four phases of inquiry:

1. *Start with Everyday Practice*
   Innovation from below begins with the challenges and opportunities that arise out of actual practice—the boring, mundane, daily activities of real classrooms. Too often, when we start with a ready-made innovation (e.g., a device, strategy, or technique) instead of everyday practice, we end up trying to implement solutions that don't correspond to meaningful problems. While it can be tempting to introduce an app or teaching method simply because it's new or because we've heard good things about it, it's a distraction if it isn't attuned to the everyday needs of our students. Always seeking out and settling for ready-made

innovations diverts our attention from building the innovations that will truly allow classrooms to thrive. The best way to identify and work toward such innovations is to begin with the classroom itself.

2. *Look for Emergent Inventions*
Once we've identified problems, frictions, or successes from practice that we would like to attend to further, the second phase of innovating from below involves looking for the already-existing solutions emerging in classrooms. Teachers and students are inventive and resourceful. When they have questions or challenges, they don't just wait for innovations to drop in from the sky; they often devise creative workarounds. However, because these workarounds are rarely valued as highly as the ready-made innovations, they are easy to overlook. Indeed, teachers and students might not even be aware of the different kinds of intuitive problem-solving they are doing each day. Innovation from below means not just paying attention to these emergent inventions but recognizing them as the foundation for more meaningful and lasting innovations for schools.

3. *Seek Out Values-Aligned Research*
The third phase involves seeking out research-based resources that enrich the emergent inventions already being used in classrooms and align with the values of educators. Even though innovation from below challenges the assumptions of the linear model's research-to-practice pipeline, it is not opposed to external research altogether. Instead, it recognizes that not all research is created equal. For this reason, it is important to seek out research that is aligned with the larger commitments of the school, its teachers, and the students and communities they serve. Taking this stance shields educators from the pressure of adopting every new innovation or "research-based" strategy that comes along. Instead, they can focus on using research to bolster and tailor on-the-ground innovations already at work in classrooms.

4. *Build Sustainable Infrastructures*
Finally, the fourth phase recognizes the importance of building infrastructures that can allow emergent, values-aligned innovations to be sustained over time. Rather than celebrating "disruption," innovation from below prioritizes the maintenance needed to keep situated classroom innovations going. This is because, unlike the linear model, this orientation recognizes that disruptions and failures do not lead inevitably to progress. Often, they create risks and instabilities that work against the interests of students. This

is another way of saying that innovation from below understands innovation not as a thing to be implemented, but an ongoing process that requires care, attention, and work to be fruitful.

THE LITERACY LAB

Over the 3 years that I managed the university–school partnership at the Innovation School, there were countless examples of administrators, teachers, and students doing innovation from below. Sometimes they implemented small, interactional innovations—the sort of daily, in-the-moment strategizing and counterstrategizing that educators attuned to their students' needs constantly and instinctively do in their classrooms. Other times, they were large, schoolwide shifts, like the introduction of the capstone Senior Showcase project.

Not all their innovations systematically went through each of the phases we have outlined, but they reflected the phases' underlying orientation. They took everyday practice as a starting point for identifying needs and desires, imagining possibilities, and creating infrastructures for meaningful, lasting, and equitable transformation. This is another way of saying that innovation from below is not a recipe or an exact science, but a *stance*—one poised in opposition to the linear approaches to innovation that tend to dominate popular discourse about education.

In what follows, we'll explore this stance by examining one of the larger and longest-lasting innovations that emerged from the Innovation School: The Literacy Lab (cf. Stornaiuolo et al., 2018). This innovation grew out of pressing needs in the school's first and second years and evolved to take on new roles and meanings as the school grew. The result was a space uniquely tuned to teachers and students, and reconciled their competing ideas about innovation in ways that no ready-made intervention could have. As we will see, this process of innovating from below was not smooth or easy, but its challenges were generative in ways that advanced educators' larger commitments to equitable teaching and learning.

Start With Everyday Practice

Even before the Innovation School opened, its stakeholders had a wide range of ideas about which ready-made innovations ought to be put to work in its classrooms. In Chapter 1, we highlighted the imaginative infrastructures of district officials, school leaders, teachers, and students that propped up technology, student autonomy, or makerspaces as what would allow the school to live up the "innovation" in its name. In all these visions for what the school might look like, a space like the Literacy Lab was never in the mix. Administrators, teachers, and students didn't anticipate it would be an innovation to implement, because the need for it emerged from within the school rather than outside of it.

The circumstances that led to the idea of the Literacy Lab began as teachers introduced features of the school makerspaces into core content-area classrooms, toward the end of the first and beginning of the second school years. Recall from earlier chapters that the educators were concerned that forms of design-oriented learning that were common in the school makerspaces were not carrying over into subjects like math, science, and humanities. They feared that students would come to see self-directed making as separate from these subjects. However, as we saw in Chapter 2, these shifts in the pedagogical infrastructures of classrooms created frictions for students. Content-area classes modeled on the makerspaces were loud and chaotic. Because students were working asynchronously, teachers sometimes struggled to keep track of who needed additional support, especially with the increased demands on students to read the dense assignment descriptions that accompanied the work-at-your-own-pace curriculum. In other words, the open-ended environment carried with it some intense literacy demands at the same time it made classrooms inhospitable to quiet, focused reading. The structure of teacher–student interaction in the spaces didn't make it easy for teachers to provide targeted reading support across content areas.

The first to recognize these problems were the school's learning support specialists. They worked closely with students who had documented reading disabilities, and they began to notice patterns in how they were struggling to navigate the increased reading demands of the making-orientated curriculum changes. Kelly, one of the learning support teachers, brought this up in a faculty meeting. She expressed concern that, in pursuing certain kinds of innovative activities, the school model was potentially overlooking its responsibility to set all students up to succeed in this environment. Put another way, the desire to be innovative was undermining essential infrastructures students depended on. Together, the teachers and research team began to discuss the wider literacy needs of the school, and what kinds of supports might be necessary for students to thrive in their classes. There was no ready-made answer to this challenge. Instead, these conversations reflected the first phase of innovation from below—starting with everyday practice. Our aim was to understand the nature of the friction that students were facing and to form a response that could meet this challenge on its own terms.

Look for Emergent Inventions

Devising a provisional solution to this challenge followed the second phase—looking for emergent inventions. We recognized that the problem we were looking to address was specific to the school context we were working in.

Even though makerspaces and asynchronous learning were popular topics in education, there were few existing models at the time for how to address challenges that arose when they were introduced into school settings. There were even fewer resources available that discussed the literacy supports that would allow such spaces to equitably serve the learning needs of all students. In other words, our impulse to look for emergent inventions partly came from the absence of external resources and solutions to apply. However, we came to appreciate that looking first to on-the-ground problem-solving opened opportunities for innovation that aren't possible when educators first look for ready-made answers.

Our process for seeking out emergent inventions involved taking stock of how students and teachers were working around the literacy challenges arising in the makerspace classrooms. In planning meetings, educators and research team members shared notes and observations from their classrooms. Gradually we began to identify a few common strategies.

We noticed that students who were having trouble focusing and reading in the makerspace classrooms were seeking refuge elsewhere. In Chapter 2, we saw one instance of this in Nadia's remaking of an empty classroom closet as a study area. Other students similarly carved out quiet work areas in hallways, or they opted to do their more focused reading activities at home.

Both research team members and teachers recognized the most useful way to support students who were struggling to navigate the asynchronous curriculum in the classroom. They provided them with structured reading strategies for making sense of the text, or simply sat with students as they read to ensure that they understood assignments and readings, and could find personally meaningful pathways into unit projects.

Educators expressed that this sort of structured support was more feasible on days when research team members were present in their classrooms. On these days, team members could circulate and answer logistical questions or sit with groups of students, freeing the teacher to do the same. In other words, teachers felt they could support students better when they had support. Obtaining support seems obvious, but is surprisingly difficult to come by in many school settings.

Students also appreciated being able to go to members of our research team when they had questions or ran into obstacles in their projects. Since the teachers were moving between check-ins, tune-ups, and conferences in the makerspace classrooms, many students were hesitant to interrupt these routines with a question. But pulling aside a research team member in the room was less intimidating.

In compiling these observations, we began to ask what infrastructures could be created that would affirm the positive developments emerging from practice, and surmount the obstacles. We distilled our notes into a few essential efforts. It was clear that we needed a *quiet space* where students could work. We also needed *targeted literacy support* for students who were struggling to make sense of instructions, assignments, and readings, or who wanted help connecting their interests to the asynchronous unit projects in the curriculum. Finally, we needed *teacher support* that would lighten the demands of teachers so they could provide instruction and coaching without feeling stretched thin or allowing some students to fly beneath their radar in the classroom.

By taking on-the-ground inventions already circulating in the school as a starting point, we had narrowed our focus to the kinds of innovations that would allow students and teachers to thrive. It now fell on us to build out these infrastructures.

Seek Out Values-Aligned Research

With several key needs and promising practices identified, we began discussing the forms of support that might be able to address one or more of them. At the time, we were not necessarily looking for a singular solution that could address all these issues. We still felt, for example, that the need for teacher support might require different responses than the need for targeted literacy instruction. We also felt the temptations of several ready-made answers to such challenges that, while research-based, were not aligned with our values and commitments. For instance, for-profit companies produce more and more technology-driven instructional resources that are sold as evidence-based solutions for personalizing learning and supporting teachers. Even though these companies can cite studies to demonstrate the effectiveness of such technologies, this kind of instruction did not line up with the teachers' own sense of what innovative teaching and learning ought to look like. Automation and data-driven efficiency can have a place in schools, but they were not our priority.

We began seeking out information about potential solutions that were backed by research that aligned with the school's and teachers' values. To do so, we invited students into a series of brainstorming meetings where we discussed what kinds of quiet learning spaces and literacy supports might be most useful to them. In these conversations, students talked about how they'd received these supports in the past from their elementary and middle school libraries. In the discussion, they mentioned missing such a space in their high school; libraries and librarian positions were among the first things eliminated during the district cuts that preceded the school's opening. Others said they loved the idea of the school makerspaces, but the noise was so distracting that they almost wished there was a "quiet makerspace" that had resources for projects but without the volume. Still others said that, while reading was a challenge in the asynchronous curriculum, it was really their *writing* that they felt was not being supported. Because they were always working at their own pace, there was rarely time to pause and think about how they wanted to approach and develop compositions.

These insights led teachers and researchers to seek out resources related to existing literatures on these subjects—libraries and library-based makerspaces, writing centers, and literacy-oriented project-based learning. Gradually, we began to see that these literatures together offered values-aligned insights that we could forge into the infrastructures of a new kind of innovation in the school. We could create a library-like space as an infrastructure for students who needed a quiet work environment. It would be open concurrent with classes so that it could support teachers, and it could provide targeted support for all of the making activities students engaged in across their classes. As the idea took shape, we began referring to it as "The Literacy Lab."

The planning of the lab was similarly a collective endeavor. Teachers, students, and research team members participated in a series of mapping exercises where we listed out ideas for potential resources, furniture, and room layouts. Cristina, a student in the school's first cohort, created a Google drawing that combined these ideas and sketched a hypothetical model for what the space might look like (Figure 4.1). Her model borrowed elements from the research literatures and sources of inspiration we had discussed, but combined them using inspiration drawn from the local context. For instance, Cristina's model included zones for independent and quiet collaborative work that echoed the design of the makerspace classrooms in the Innovation School. This would allow the room to feel like it was separate from, yet continuous with, the structures at work throughout the Innovation School.

One side effect of following this process of designing the Literacy Lab—that is, not dropping in a ready-made solution, but building it "from below"—was that teachers and students recognized it as an outgrowth of *their* experiences and efforts. They felt a tremendous amount

Figure 4.1. Recreation of Cristina's map of the Literacy Lab.

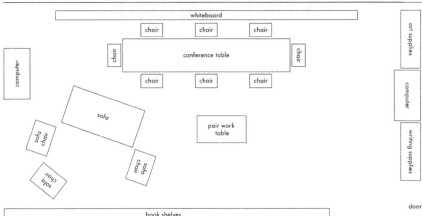

of ownership over the innovation, which can't be said as easily for much of what passes for innovation in schools today. By the time we had found a location for the Lab and secured the necessary resources through donations and a small grant, the enthusiasm for the space was palpable. On the day the books, shelves, tables, and chairs for the Lab were to be delivered, students asked to stay after school to begin assembling the space rather than waiting until the following day. Teachers, too, joined in the impromptu construction party, and before long the space so many people imagined together began to materialize into one they could inhabit and use (Figure 4.2).

Satisfyingly, and not at all coincidentally, the entire process aligned with the larger vision of the school. In an interview, Kelly, the school's learning support teacher, explained that she saw it as an extension of the school's focus on design-thinking:

> The Lit Lab, to me, has very much been part of the design-thinking process. . . . Educators collaborate and now students are collaborating. It's gone through several prototypes. We're getting user feedback. All of that is intertwined. . . .

Figure 4.2. Students and teachers building the Literacy Lab. (Photos taken by members of the research team.)

Our school is in a design process. I mean, it's such a big part of who we are and really makes us unique.

Her words suggest that what emerged from this process was not just an easy application of a ready-made innovation. Rather, it grew organically out of the particularities and contingencies of the school itself, and the values of its teachers and students. Using these as a starting point and a guide, rather than an afterthought, was important to shaping the innovation that surfaced as a result.

Build Sustainable Infrastructures

From the first days after it opened, the Literacy Lab proved to be a tremendous resource. Because it had been developed to address the specific needs of students and teachers, it fit snugly into the routines unfolding throughout the school. When students were having difficulty concentrating on an assignment or if they needed targeted support, they could request to go to the Literacy Lab. At the lab, members of our research team were available to help or ensure that the room remained a focused environment. Members of our team also continued to meet with teachers regularly so that we remained informed about the activities happening in each class, so that we could better support students. Even students who did not require a quiet workplace would drop into the Lab during their breaks to sign out a book from the library or to pick up project materials for an assignment they were working on. However, despite the success of the Literacy Lab, it was not yet a sustainable resource.

We knew, for instance, that the Lab depended on our research team members being available to staff it. While our partnership with the school was a long-term relationship, it would not last forever. Because the partnership was temporary, we recognized there would be a longitudinal need to develop infrastructures that would allow the most fruitful aspects of the Literacy Lab to go on long after our formal partnership ended. What we did not anticipate was that there would be more immediate sustainability needs to address. Even before we could confront the challenge of setting up the Lab to succeed beyond the length of our university–school partnership, we would need to configure the Lab to support the more mundane evolutions that occurred in the classrooms.

While teachers, students, and researchers had worked together to design the Literacy Lab in response to several experienced challenges, those challenges did not remain stable. Schools are living environments, and as new students, teachers, and resources enter into them, they are reshaped accordingly. This is one of the reasons why so many ready-made innovations fail. Because they aren't tailored to the schools where they are introduced, they are incapable of adapting to the unpredictable shifts that inevitably occur as educators and students engage in the work of teaching and learning. While innovations designed from below—tuned to the everyday needs of classrooms—fare better, they too require adaptation. Thinking infrastructurally about innovation cannot stop once an idea has been designed and implemented; it must continue to attend to the maintenance of these innovations. Maintenance means continually reflecting on the relationship between an innovation and its use, and on the infrastructures that must be reinforced or altered to ensure that the guiding values and commitments that went into the making of that innovation continue to be served.

Throughout the Innovation School's second year, the need for a quiet workspace where students could get targeted literacy support persisted. However, as students and faculty saw the space being used, they began to imagine new possibilities for it. These uses would lead to transformations of the space that exceeded our initial plans. The leader of the Community Organizing Makerspace, for instance, had long wanted to invite community members to the school for students to conduct interviews about the neighborhood and its history. This Literacy Lab afforded space and resources for such exchanges. Students had also been pushing the principal to allow more student-led clubs in the school, which were prevented by space restrictions. With the Literacy Lab open, this created room for electives to form. A book club, a creative writing club, a video game design club, and even a dance team began to meet in the Literacy Lab at lunch and after school on different days of the week.

Several of these uses pushed the limits of how the space had originally been envisioned, which occasionally resulted in frictions. Some teachers worried that the more informal gathering in the Lab might muddy its association with quiet work during class time. Likewise, the students who contributed to the design of the Lab sometimes felt territorial about changes in the room's configurations—particularly when these changes were initiated by students who came to the school *after* the Lab had already been opened. These tensions prompted conversations between our research team members, teachers, and students about what aspects of an innovation ought to change or be preserved once it has been introduced to the world and took on a life of its own. Ultimately, we determined that the best guide for decisions and changes in the space was not fidelity to our original designs, but to the values that inspired those designs. In the case of the Literacy Lab, our commitment was to all students feeling that they had a place where they could work in a focused environment, could get targeted support for their creative and academic projects, and where resources for them to succeed were readily available. Using these principles as a metric for the success of the space allowed different stakeholders to let go of the need to control the space, and instead to see how it could best serve those who used it.

Adapting the Literacy Lab to meet new and evolving needs at the school, even as it remained rooted in its guiding values, was a powerful way that we were able to build and reinforce infrastructures for the space to last. But the challenge remained to ensure that the Lab could endure when there were no longer research team members to staff it. To address this, teachers suggested that we invite students to begin serving as peer coaches in the lab space. At first, our team was hesitant; students at the school already had plenty of other responsibilities. We did not want to increase their workloads just to keep the Literacy Lab open. But as conversations continued, administrators and teachers noted that the competency-based model could allow students who wished to participate in the peer-coaching program to earn credits if they met with teachers to document and discuss their coaching. When we invited students into these discussions, they were enthusiastic. Many were already participating in book clubs and writing clubs in the Lab, and the idea of getting credit to help their classmates appealed to them.

The Writing Fellows program was launched from these discussions. Any student who wanted to be a Writing Fellow would talk to their teacher and then be invited to participate in a series of training workshops. When the program began, our research team led these workshops, talking to students about how to give feedback on peers' work and practicing holding conferences with one another. After completing the training, students could then sign up for time slots where they would serve as peer coaches in the Lab. Our research team members were there to assist them. Gradually, our support was able to become more hands-off as students felt more confident in their abilities as coaches. By the start of the third year, the Writing Fellows program had been formalized, and Fellows would hold regular meetings with teachers and research team members to discuss their successes and challenges in the Lab and to offer advice to one another. By the fourth year, the program was almost entirely run by students and a teacher advisor. The Writing Fellows program now was a crucial sustaining infrastructure that would allow the Lab to continue into the future.

BUILDING INFRASTRUCTURES FOR EQUITY

The example of the Literacy Lab reveals features of the process of innovating from below that set it apart from the linear model commonly used in schools and that highlight its potentials for supporting more equitable teaching and learning.

Embracing Values-Driven Iteration

The first point is the significance of *values-driven iteration.* Iteration is a central concept in the linear model of innovation. It's the idea that change happens through recurring cycles of tinkering and adapting, which eventually lead to improved outcomes. The problem with this understanding of "iteration," however, is that it assumes a linear path toward progress. When we implement a new ready-made technology or teaching strategy, we are often told that adapting to it will eventually lead to it becoming an organic part of our everyday practice. But not everything that we can iteratively adapt to is necessarily an improvement to our instruction, much less to our students' learning. If iteration is unmoored from the values that drive us to do what we do, then it can easily lead us astray.

The success of the Literacy Lab was only possible because we began the process of building this innovation by focusing on our values as educators. It was our commitment to equitable student flourishing that allowed us to recognize, in the first place, the problems that students were facing in the classrooms. This same commitment animated our efforts to design infrastructures that could better support all students—by looking for emergent inventions already at work in the school and seeking out resources and research that aligned with our desire for equitable education.

The ability of the Literacy Lab to evolve with the changing needs of the school and to establish new programs to allow the program to persist without depending on our research team were examples of values-driven iteration. In these moments of transition, teachers, researchers, and students had opportunities to reflect on their commitments and determine whether their iterative responses would preserve the innovation we had envisioned or the underlying values that led us to envision it. In other words, these values served as a guide for how iterative innovation ought to unfold, and what kinds of infrastructures might be necessary to build or adapt to sustain that innovation into the future.

Moving From Practice to Research (and Back Again)

The second point of the process of innovation from below in the Literacy Lab relates to the role of research in equitable educational practice. The Lab illustrates the powerful possibilities that reveal themselves when we conceptualize innovation as cultivated through everyday practices, emergent inventions, values-aligned research, and sustainable infrastructures. Innovations from above rarely offer such assurances. If you were to try to implement the exact model of the Literacy Lab I've described above into your own school or classroom, you would not find the same results. Local contingencies would shape what such an innovation from below would look like. With that said, if you were to go through the phases of innovating from below, then it would absolutely be possible for you to find values-aligned resources in the Literacy Lab that could inspire your own on-the-ground innovating. The innovation itself is not—and should never be—the point; it's the stance that we take toward innovation that matters.

Realizing that our stance toward innovation matters is both intimidating and freeing. It is intimidating because it means we must abandon the comforting untruth that ready-made innovations will save us. But it is also freeing because it eliminates the pressure that administrators and teachers often feel to seek out new gadgets or flashy teaching techniques. Instead, we can focus on the innovations that matter most—those that serve the situated needs of students.

Put another way, innovating from below flips the research-to-practice pipeline on its head by centering practice as a starting point for seeking out research solutions that align with our guiding values. This is not to downplay the role of research, but rather to reframe it. Indeed, over the years since the Innovation School's Literacy Lab and its Writing Fellows program started, teachers and students have presented at practice-oriented and research conferences, and even published research articles based on their work (e.g., Plummer et al., 2020).

By wresting innovation from the domain of outside experts and product developers, innovating from below invites educators to rethink the relationship between research and practice and their own place within that relationship. In doing so, it opens opportunities for transformative teaching and learning nurtured through lived classroom experiences. Ready-made innovation, no matter how bold its promises, can never fulfill this possibility.

Conclusion

A More Ambitious Innovation

Throughout this book, we have explored the competing interests and imperatives that shape how "innovation" gets imagined, invoked, and implemented in today's schools. Several themes have surfaced and resurfaced about the implications of innovation for educational equity:

- First, *innovation, as it is commonly used in education, privileges national-economic and corporate interests over those of schools and communities.* We have seen this, for instance, in the way that certain imaginative infrastructures associated with innovation prioritized the concerns of policymakers and philanthropic actors over those of students and teachers (Chapter 1). It also occurs when technological infrastructures tether teaching and learning to commercial logics with different values from those of educators (Chapter 3).
- Second, *the imperative to "disrupt" education is incompatible with efforts to build sustainable infrastructures for equitable teaching and learning.* This is evident, for example, when new innovations that promise to "modernize" schools work against already existing pedagogical infrastructures in classrooms that teachers and students depend on (Chapter 2).
- Third, *the impacts of innovation fall unevenly on stakeholders.* We have repeatedly seen how the same innovations that serve the needs of some create new challenges and complications for others. Those who are most insulated from the risks and costs of disruption are given an advantage. Those who aren't insulated can, in the most troubling instances, be made to feel personally responsible for an innovation's systemic shortcomings.
- Fourth, *relocating innovation in the lived dynamics of schools can mobilize alternate approaches to school transformation.* By starting with everyday practice as a site for innovation, it becomes possible to "innovate from below"—building sustainable infrastructures, driven by schools' and educators' commitments to equity and student flourishing (Chapter 4).

102

Taken together, these themes clarify the potential of innovation from below as an interpretive and affirmative frame for thinking about educational innovation. It is *interpretive* because it offers resources for analyzing new and existing innovations. These resources include mapping how innovations work and for whom, identifying frictions in and among their infrastructures (and the infrastructures of other innovations already embedded in classrooms), and addressing their uneven impacts on students. It is also *affirmative* because it suggests an alternate, more proactive approach to innovation. If "innovation" is to be more than a buzzword—if it is to positively contribute to the project of equitable public education—it will require more than just critical analysis. We need a different way to innovate, an innovation that begins with a commitment to equity and the public good, and that marshals analysis and critique toward building infrastructures that will uphold these values. This is the affirmative project to which innovation from below aspires.

To this point, our exploration of these interpretive and affirmative potentials has been grounded in the Innovation School. In concluding, I want to suggest that these lessons have implications that go beyond this particular school. In fact, these lessons extend to any public schools that desire to be innovative or that find themselves uncomfortably caught in the din and rush of the linear model's imperatives to "disrupt" education. While there were many particularities involved in the building of the Innovation School, the wider pressures that teachers and students faced share family resemblances with those now experienced in the making of "innovative" schools or classrooms everywhere. As such, the Innovation School offers powerful lessons not only about the limits of the linear model, but also how we might adopt a different view of educational transformation—one that starts not with ready-made solutions, but with attention to the infrastructures of innovation.

SEEING INNOVATION INFRASTRUCTURALLY

Infrastructure is everywhere and nowhere. The roads we drive on, the bridges we cross, the pipelines that bring us water and carry away waste—all this infrastructure surrounds us. It is only through the smooth interoperation of these infrastructures that we are able to go about our lives without paying much attention to them. As independent as we'd like to believe we are, our social existence is upheld by dense networks of interoperable infrastructures. Most often, it is only when these relations break down—when infrastructures announce themselves to us—that we are jarred to realize how reliant we are on them.

We have seen examples of infrastructural breakdown in recent years, when many have viscerally felt the profound uncertainties that follow when critical infrastructures are torn from us or allowed to erode. In the aftermath of the 2016 United States presidential election, which occurred during my work with the Innovation School, sudden changes and instabilities in institutions, policies, and guidelines—each a form of infrastructure—exposed students and teachers to new forms of risk and harm. Almost immediately at the Innovation School, conversations in faculty meetings shifted from pedagogical matters to crisis management. Students, especially those who were Black, Latinx, undocumented, or Muslim, expressed fears about their families' safety. In the absence of protections from federal, state, or city governments, it fell to the school and its teachers to build provisional, ad hoc infrastructures to help their students feel safe, even as many faculty and staff members also felt the pinch of increased precarity.

The COVID-19 pandemic similarly exposed the significance of global health and education infrastructure. The rapid shift to virtual learning in the spring of 2020 revealed vast inequities in students' access to basic infrastructures like a working computer and home Internet connection. It also laid bare the surprising dependencies that many schools already had on third-party commercial platforms that allowed them to make this pivot (cf. Garcia & Nichols, 2021). Education technology scholars argue that the tech industry seized on the pandemic to further establish themselves as critical infrastructures for teaching and learning across countries and age levels (Perrotta, 2020; Williamson, 2020). Likewise, the pressure to reopen schools in the United States—often before it was safe to do so—spotlighted how many public schools function as a basic infrastructure for wider social systems. They allow society to run smoothly, providing not only educational development but also childcare, meals, health care, counseling, and other social services that might otherwise be inaccessible to students and their families.

Seeing infrastructurally, as I have tried to do throughout this book, attunes our attention to these relations that often sit just below the surface of observable school and classroom practices. Innovations in technology or policy or physical spaces always carry with them assumptions, interests, and values that do not just go away when they are grafted onto a new setting. These features reshape the infrastructures of that setting, leading to uneven and unanticipated consequences. Identifying and addressing shifts and frictions in these infrastructures are essential to building educational innovations oriented toward equity.

THE INNOVATION GOSPEL

Of course, this is easier said than done. The challenge of seeing innovation infrastructurally is that it goes against the linear view of innovation that is so predominant and persuasive that it is taken for granted in schools. Throughout this book, we have drawn out the contrasts between the linear view and innovating from below. We have seen the shortcomings and dangers of the former, and we have highlighted the potentials of the latter. What we have not talked about is *why* the linear model, for all its flaws, persists as a foundational explanation for how innovation works. It would be easy to write its dominance off as naivety. However, as enchanted as people can be with the sheen of new "innovative" things, deep down they know (and have likely personally experienced) the failures of innovation. Even the Cold War scientists who helped establish the linear model and benefitted from large government investments in innovative research and development were uncertain about the framework. After all, it's hard to build an atomic bomb, watch its devastating aftereffects, and still regard scientific and technological development as the sole cause of moral and human progress.

I want to suggest that the lure of the linear model comes not from ignorance, but from the fact that it is useful. People—even those well aware of its shortcomings—are drawn to the idea because it does real work for them. In a world of complexity and confusion, pain and suffering, it offers a hopeful promise: that things will continue to improve. Even more, it offers a concrete assurance that we can participate in this improvement if we only commit to riding out the instabilities as "the new" is born out of the disruption of "the old." This is another way of saying that the linear model is compelling enough for people to overlook its limitations because it offers a powerful and empowering story about how social transformation happens. It's a good news story, a story of salvation—which is why I call it *the Innovation Gospel.*

My use of this phrase derives from economist W. Norton Grubb and historian Marvin Lazerson's influential concept of "the education gospel." For Grubb and Lazerson (2004), the *education gospel* refers to the cycle of critique and affirmation that underpins the belief in schooling as an unequivocal good. The story begins with the damnation of school as-it-is: that classrooms, teaching methods, and technologies are outmoded and unfit for 21st-century learning. It concludes by highlighting school as-it-could-be: that is, how aligning the curriculum to the needs of the 21st-century workforce can lead to economic, social, and individual salvation for students, communities, and even entire nations. The education gospel encourages the repetition of this cycle, meaning that schools are perpetually being optimized to serve market interests, and students have little choice but to keep the faith and pursue education. They fear being left behind, even as the goalposts for credentialling and upward mobility shift.

From this description, we can begin to see how the innovation and education gospels are related. On one hand, the education gospel is a subset of the innovation gospel. Education, after all, is not the only sector in which we encounter such salvation stories, where the outmoded and antiquated are made anew through market optimization and disruption. In recent years, we have seen the gospel of innovation deployed to modernize everything from colleges (MOOCs), transportation (rideshares), and law enforcement (predictive policing) to health care (self-tracking software). Yet the innovation gospel also depends on the education gospel. Those insistent on optimizing and modernizing different sectors of society rely on schools to continue to produce new generations of workers who can keep these changing sectors afloat. The two faiths, in innovation and in education, are entangled; a near-religious belief in their goodness enwraps both.

The trouble, as Grubb and Lazerson argue, is that blind faith in the education gospel—and by extension, the innovation gospel—reinforces inequity. It does so in three ways, which we have seen evidence of throughout this book. The first is that *it shifts attention away from the material conditions of schooling, teaching, and learning, and toward the external optimizations and quick fixes that promise deliverance*. It is oriented toward dropping in solutions from above, rather than understanding the problems as they are and potential of practices from below. In many ways, the Innovation School's origin story itself is an example of this. Recall that in the years leading up to the school's opening, the district had shuttered dozens of neighborhood schools. Parents and students had led protests amid the closures and budget cuts calling for increased school funding. It is telling that in this combative environment, the most readily available response that the school district could imagine was not a reinvestment in neighborhood programs, but the institution of a new "innovative" school. The lure of the innovation gospel is such that it shapes how educators and administrators see and address problems. Officials would sooner create a novel, disruptive innovation than care for the existing, if fractured, resources that serve the common good.

It is also telling that parents, students, and teachers gravitated to the Innovation School at all. Organizing and protests that led to the school's opening demanded equitable investments in public schools, not "more innovation." The school was untested, and its innovative model wasn't even fully formed when its doors opened. What would possess people to sign their children up to be part of such an experiment? Their enthusiasm is related to the second way that the innovation gospel reinforces inequity: *It uses the promise of a potential upside to encourage people to absorb risk*. Scholars of innovation and innovative industries have long documented this downside of optimism. Anthropologist Gina Neff, in her study of tech workers in New York's Silicon Alley (Neff, 2012), found that most people took these risky jobs with long hours and little stability because they saw *all* work—including more conventional employment options—becoming riskier. They were comfortable trading current workplace conditions for new and unfamiliar ones because there was a higher ceiling for success if the risk happened to pay off. We can see a similar effect in education. When public schools are underfunded, teachers are underpaid, resources are scarce, and narratives about "failing" programs abound, parents, students, and teachers come to expect less stability and support from schools. In turn, they comply with working under more precarious conditions. In this way, the innovation gospel perpetuates inequity by offloading risk onto the very publics to whom schools are meant to provide dependable services and durable working conditions.

A third way that the innovation gospel contributes to educational inequity is by *shifting risk from institutions to people, creating a mechanism for blaming individuals for the systemic failures of "innovation."* There have been times, for instance, when I have presented research from the Innovation School at conferences and professional workshops and attendees have been quick to point out what they perceive to be faults or shortcomings in the way that its teachers implemented particular innovative practices. Perhaps you, in reading about some of the challenges that surfaced in the early years of the Innovation School, had a similar response. If only the principal had done X, or if the teachers had done Y, then innovation Z would have worked as it was supposed to. The inclination to look for people to blame rather than systems to reform is what makes the innovation gospel run. It pushes responsibility downward, because when innovations don't live up to their promises, districts can blame administrators, administrators can blame teachers, and teachers can blame students. All the while, what goes unexamined is why the larger systems have produced and upheld particular understandings of and assumptions about innovation. Those who design and market "innovative" solutions merely address the problems these theories of innovation perpetuated in the first place. The truth is that the administrators, teachers, and students I worked with at the Innovation School were some of the most brilliant, talented, creative, and compassionate people I have encountered in my career as an educator. They were also constrained by systems that perpetually pressured them to seek external innovations, even when it went against their better instincts. This is not to say there wasn't powerful and transformative work that happened in the school; we've seen examples to the contrary throughout this book. But those transformations happened in spite of, not because of, the linear model of innovation that animated the systems they worked within. In other words, the innovation gospel perpetuates inequity by impeding on-the-ground innovation tuned to the needs of communities, even as it places responsibility for those unmet needs back onto those working within the compromised systems that the gospel helped create.

A MORE AMBITIOUS INNOVATION

In one sense, we can understand the Innovation Gospel as telling a story about innovation that is too large. It presents innovation as an autonomous, independent force leading through the stages of the linear model, toward progress. In doing so, it misses the smaller details about how innovations get made and put to work by real people in real settings, leading to real consequences. But in another sense, the Innovation Gospel also tells a story about innovation that is too small. Because it conceptualizes "innovations" as individual artifacts and practices—like a new technology, teaching method, or organizational strategy—it can easily fail to account for some of the largest, most ambitious innovations that humans have ever developed. Indeed, some of these innovations have been so successful that it's easy not to recognize them as "innovations" any longer. We simply take them for granted.

One such innovation is public education itself. If we step back and think about it, the idea of offering free and accessible schooling to every child, regardless of background, is an outrageous proposition. Offering education in places as linguistically, racially, religiously, and economically diverse as those in the global North is ambitious. Even more, to not just suggest the idea in theory, but to actually *build* it—that's pretty wild. Public education is so ambitious, in fact, I'd venture that if the public education system weren't already in place today, and someone were to propose it, it would not only go unfunded, but the proposer would be mocked for their unrealistic, pie-in-the-sky dreaming. Like other public resources we take for granted today—public libraries, public parks, public transportation, public health clinics, and public arts programs—public education only exists because people before us saw it as worthwhile to fight for innovations that serve the common good, not just personal interests or the market.

That fight has not been an easy one. People in dominant positions and groups have battled to limit the public served by public education only to those who look, talk, believe, and behave as they do. When activists, agitators, and lawyers have fought for protections to ensure that education was accessible and equitable for all students, dominant groups poured resources into gutting, dismantling, and disparaging the innovation of public education. In *The Wolf at the Schoolhouse Door* (2020), Jack Schneider and Jennifer Berkshire document this history by showing how politicians, corporations, and edupreneurs incrementally undermined public education— the most ambitious educational innovation ever attempted. They persuaded people that a parade of short-lived, market-driven solutions (e.g., charter schools, voucher programs, personalized learning technologies) were the *real* innovations we ought to be investing in.

Though there is a colossal gulf between these competing visions of innovation, the Innovation Gospel sometimes makes it difficult to see the incongruity. The linear model of innovation draws our attention to what is new and what we are told is an improvement. Within this logic, the individual-oriented, market-driven solutions on offer to administrators, teachers, and students can look and feel a lot like progress. This is why we find even fierce advocates of public education like the teachers at the Innovation School buying into and perpetuating the narrative that schools are antiquated institutions, in dire need of modernization with new tools, techniques, and organizational strategies. Such charges place the locus of change on "modernization," not the larger need for public schools to support the flourishing of all students, irrespective of market demands. Public schools aren't perfect, and they have yet to live up to the heights of their promise to be equitable institutions. However, whenever our efforts to reform public schools are directed toward "modernization" and not justice, we are replacing the more ambitious potential of public education as an innovation for the common good with a narrower one.

What an infrastructural view of innovation offers us is a set of resources for clarifying the differences between these views of innovation. Rather than taking claims about technological or pedagogical progress at face value, viewing innovation from below invites us to ask, "Progress for whom, and toward what end?" If we recognize equitable public education itself as one of the most ambitious innovations educators can strive for, a different test for evaluating the claims of new innovations begins to crystallize. From this view, it no longer makes sense to weigh an innovation by its costs and benefits. Rather, it is most sensibly weighed by its potential to contribute to the larger goal of making schools more equitable places for teachers to work and for students to learn. Such an orientation flips the linear model on its head; when we see public education as an innovation, then the work of improving it should not be a matter of disruption, but one of repair.

THE INNOVATION OF REPAIR

We probably don't immediately associate *repair* with innovation. The word "repair" usually conjures a process of restoring a damaged object to an earlier, unbroken state. It is, in a sense, about returning to the past. Innovation—or, the version the linear model has popularized, at least—appears to be the opposite of this: a break from the past that ushers in a new future. But just as we have already seen that this linear view is not the only way to understand "innovation," so too is this restorative view of "repair" not the only way we might think about the term. Indeed, the architect Christopher Alexander argues that repair can be a radical project. In his book *The Timeless Way of Building* (1979), he suggests that repair is not just a restorative process, but a speculative one. Repair is the work of mending or amending the world, or created objects within it, to bring them to their full potential. Repairing a building, for Alexander, does not mean fixing its superficial problems, but attending to the infrastructures that prevent it from achieving its fullest possibilities.

Recently, this sense of repair has gained attention in research focused on the often invisible care and maintenance work that society depends on but rarely acknowledges. In 2016, a group of scholars began hosting an annual conference called "The Maintainers" (www.maintainers.org) to draw attention to the fact that, even though we live in a world that celebrates the rapidity of innovation and disruption, it is the patient, material work of maintenance that keeps things running. Like Alexander, these scholars recognize "repair" and "maintenance" not in the conventional sense of preserving things as they are or restoring them to how they were. Maintenance of roadway infrastructures, for instance, often involves dramatic excisions of old or faulty work. Repairing these systems, in other words, involves not just studying and detecting these problems through careful attention to how they are (or aren't) working. It also involves building new infrastructures that will allow them to serve their original purpose even better than their previous design allowed them to.

This vision of repair is akin to the approach to innovation we have explored in this book. If, as we have said, equitable public education is one of the most ambitious innovations we can strive for, then taking a reparative stance is a radical and progressive project. It involves studying and identifying the infrastructures that work with or against the promise of equitable public schooling. It means protecting those infrastructures from outside forces and influences that might corrode or reshape them so that they no longer serve their purpose. Further, it also might require us to mend or build new infrastructures to replace those that are not upholding public education's ambitious vision for student flourishing. An orientation of repair helps to ground innovation in the values and aims to which it aspires. Where the Innovation Gospel strives for "progress" as an end in itself, innovation from below understands progress is meaningless if unmoored from a larger vision for repair.

This doesn't mean that we entirely ignore ready-made innovations. Instead, we weigh those innovations with attention to how they live up to the values and promise of equitable public education. An orientation toward repair shields educators from the pressures to adopt and adapt to whatever the next innovation-of-the-day is. It encourages them to invest in shaping or creating those that will serve our students and the common good. If this proposal sounds modest or conservative, it is worth remembering that it is these innovations from below that have led to the most substantive and material improvements to schools over the last century. Trends have come and gone, but the innovations that have secured durable infrastructures to sustain and support teachers' working conditions and students' learning conditions are the ones that have been so influential that we often take them for granted. As educational historians David Tyack and Larry Cuban note in their sweeping history of U.S. school reform, *Tinkering Toward Utopia* (1995),

> Other innovations, once deliberate reforms, became so pervasive that they were no longer seen as reforms and thus disappeared from the scoreboard of successful changes. Indoor plumbing, central heating, and blackboards are examples.

They may seem trivial, hardly worth the label of reforms, yet not long ago they were high on the agenda of necessary innovations. (p. 54)

We can add other innovations to this list that are similarly taken for granted today, yet only exist because people before us were willing to fight uphill battles to secure them for future generations: hot lunches, summer school, teacher unions, community centers, kindergartens, school nurses, sex education, playgrounds, and after-school recreation. They may not make for flashy TED Talks or showstopping speeches on school tours with prospective students, but it's innovations like these that provide the infrastructures that allow schools to live up to their potential. Neglecting infrastructure allows the visionary possibilities of public education to fail, leaving them vulnerable to the pressure of individual and market interests. But when we devote ourselves to the care-work of mending, reinforcing, and building anew such infrastructures, we are joining in a powerful collective project. We are walking arm in arm with the generations of educators, communities, activists, and students who believed that there were greater innovations to strive for, and grander possibilities for how education might serve society.

RETHINKING THE "INNOVATION SCHOOL"

Over the 3 years that I partnered with the Innovation School, I learned a great deal about what innovation means, how it works, who it serves, why it fails, and how imagining it otherwise might open new possibilities for equitable public education. In this book, I have tried to distill these lessons from the Innovation School in such a way that they offer insights for other "innovation schools"—those that explicitly aspire to be innovative, or feel the pressures of cultural imperatives for innovating and disrupting. We've explored several frameworks for thinking about the infrastructures of innovation: the *imaginative* infrastructures that shape how different stakeholders think about it; the *pedagogical* infrastructures that are reconfigured when innovations are implemented into classrooms; and the *technological* infrastructures that introduce the design decisions of distant actors into the local settings of our schools. We have also considered the affirmative possibilities that an infrastructural view of innovation might hold. By beginning with everyday practice, we can build infrastructures for on-the-ground innovations that serve our own and our students needs better than the ready-made offerings marketed to us.

As counterintuitive as the ways we've examined innovation here might seem, the underlying conclusion is an old (and perhaps even an obvious) one: Transformative teaching and learning do not come from ready-made solutions. They come from faithful attention to the needs, identities, desires, and dreams of students and communities, and a commitment to equitable education for the common good. To the extent that the sheen of new innovations distract us from these purposes, they are useless; and to the extent that they serve these ends, they are worth nurturing and sustaining. In this way, innovation from below is an orientation closely allied with other traditions of education research and practice that similarly recognize that the location from which we theorize innovation matters (Ghiso et al., 2013). Rich literatures of teacher research, action research, practitioner inquiry, and participatory research have shown that innovations are not just passed down from university labs, industry, or edupreneurs. Innovations are cultivated through the lived dynamics of schools, classrooms, and teacher–student interaction (Cochran-Smith & Lytle, 2009). The insights that follow from such perspectives tell us that innovating from below has widespread implications across educational settings:

- *For practitioners*, it suggests we need to analyze the innovations that are presented to us as ready-made resources and to weigh them in relation to the more ambitious innovation that drives our work—the promise of joyful and equitable public education. New technologies, teaching strategies, and classroom organization techniques—even those that seem innocuous, or unequivocally good—are never neutral. They bring assumptions and values that may affect our interests and those of our students. They may reconfigure our schools in ways that compromise the existing infrastructures our classrooms depend on. But even more, innovation from below also suggests the need to go beyond analysis alone, to recognize everyday practice as a site where powerful innovations are born. Schools and classrooms are not just testing sites for other people's research and development agendas; they are spaces of emergent invention. If innovation is to have any place in the nurturing of equitable teaching and learning, it will begin with practice.

- *For school- and district-level educational leaders*, viewing innovation from below demands that we take seriously the real needs of teachers and students, and the forms of on-the-ground innovation they are *already* engaged in. Too often, well-meaning principals and district leaders gravitate to ready-made solutions because they promise a convenient way to address systemic challenges. It is comforting to believe that purchasing new technologies or instituting a new professional learning structure will set our schools down a linear path toward progress. But ready-made innovations offer no such assurances. Even worse, the interests and imperatives embedded in them may actually lead away from the only real measure of progress that truly matters— the flourishing of our students. Looking to the everyday work of classrooms as a starting point for innovation offers an alternative, because it clarifies the considerations that might go into decisions about spending and policy. Rather than looking first for external solutions, we might ask instead: What infrastructures—material resources, time, or protective policies—might nurture classroom environments in which teachers feel encouraged, empowered, and supported to lean into the everyday innovating they are already doing? They should know that these ideas will be taken just as seriously as those parachuted into schools from above, if not, indeed, more so.

- *For researchers,* innovation from below involves a similar shift in perspective. Researchers have been beneficiaries of the assumption, embedded in the linear model, that innovations travel "from research to practice." Every year millions of dollars are allocated to university labs and industry R&D departments for developing and testing new teaching and learning innovations. This momentum shows no signs of slowing down. Even when these innovations falter or fail, the Innovation Gospel delivers new streams of funding to study these failures and to propose solutions to them. This is not necessarily a bad thing, as important studies and resources have emerged from this research. But innovation from below offers a different perspective on such investments. As we have seen, not everything that emerges through the research-to-practice pipeline serves the interests of teachers, students, and the long-term viability of public education for the common good. Further, well-meaning and soundly designed research can still be easily appropriated and misused. Researchers, then, have a responsibility to think carefully about how their work contributes to perpetuating the Innovation Gospel, and how they might use the resources available to them to support forms of innovation that are rooted in classrooms and a vision for equitable public education. One way of doing this might include partnering with teachers and students to share and amplify such work. Such partnerships might not lead to insights that can become ready-made innovations to be dropped into new settings. Rather, they might model the kinds of ingenuity that emerge when we take seriously the innovation already at work in our schools and classrooms.

Across these groups of stakeholders—teachers, administrators, and researchers—we can see possibilities open when we shift the locus of innovation, seeing it not as something to be dropped into public schools, but as something that emerges from them. These possibilities are attached to everyday practices of teaching and learning, and an ambitious commitment to an equitable education as a public good. When rooted in such values, the meaning of innovation shifts. It is not a linear process of disrupting teaching and learning as we know them to make room for the new. Rather, it is a reparative stance that starts with attention to and care for the material conditions of real schools, real teachers, and real students. It works to imagine, mend, and build the infrastructures needed to reach and sustain the promise of public education—not with ready-made solutions dropped from above, but with those nurtured through everyday practice from below.

References

Alexander, C. (1979). *The timeless way of building*. Oxford University Press.

Ames, M. (2019, October 18). The smartest people in the room? What Silicon Valley's supposed obsession with tech-free private schools really tells us. *LA Review of Books*. https://www.lareviewofbooks.org/article/the-smartest-people-in-the-room-what-silicon-valleys-supposed-obsession-with-tech-free-private-schools-really-tells-us/

Anagnostopoulos, D, Rutledge, S. A., & Jacobsen, R. (2013). *The infrastructure of accountability: Data use and the transformation of American education*. Harvard Education Press.

Anand, N., Gupta, A., & Appel, G. (2020). *The promise of infrastructure*. Duke University Press.

Anderson, J. (1987). *The education of Blacks in the South, 1860–1935*. North Carolina University Press.

Anderson, W. (2006). *Colonial pathologies: American tropical medicine, race, and hygiene in the Philippines*. Duke University Press.

Anyon, J. (1980). Social class and the hidden curriculum of work. *The Journal of Education, 162*(1), 67–92.

Appadurai, A. (1990). Disjuncture and difference in the global cultural economy. *Theory, Culture, & Society, 7*, 295–310.

Atwell, N. (1987). *In the middle: reading, writing, and learning from adolescents*. Heinemann.

Benjamin, R. (2019). *Race after technology: Abolitionist tools for the new Jim Code*. Polity.

Benkler, Y. (2007). *The wealth of networks: How social production transforms markets and freedom*. Yale University Press.

Bowker, G.C., & Star, S.L. (1999). *Sorting things out: Classification and its consequences*. The MIT Press.

Bowles, S., & Gintis, H. (1976). *Schooling in capitalist America: Educational reform and the contradictions of economic life*. Basic Books.

Brooks, M., & Lasser, J. (2018). *Tech generation: Raising balanced kids in a hyper-connected world*. Oxford University Press.

Buras, K. L. (2015). *Charter schools, race, and urban space: Where the market meets grassroots resistance*. Routledge.

Bush, V. (1945). *Science: The endless frontier*. Ayer Co.

Campano, G., Ghiso, M. P., & Welch, B. (2016). *Partnering with immigrant communities: Action through literacy*. Teachers College Press.

Carr, N. (2008). Is Google making us stupid? *The Atlantic*. https://www.theatlantic.com/magazine/archive/2008/07/is-google-making-us-stupid/306868/

Chakrabarty, D. (1998). Minority histories, subaltern pasts. *Postcolonial Studies, 1*(1), 15–29.

Chakrabarty, D. (2009). The climate of history: Four theses. *Critical Inquiry, 35*(2), 197–222.

Christensen, C. (1997). *The innovator's dilemma: When new technologies cause great firms to fail*. Harvard Business Review Press.

Christensen, C., Horn, M., & Johnson, C. (2008). *Disrupting class: How disruptive innovation will change the way the world learns*. McGraw-Hill.

Christensen, C., & Raynor, M. (2003). *The innovator's solution: Creating and sustaining successful growth*. Harvard Business Review Press.

Cochran-Smith, M., & Lytle, S. (2009). *Inquiry as stance: Practitioner research for the next generation*. Teachers College Press.

Collins, A. M., & Halverson, R. (2018). *Rethinking education in the age of technology: The digital revolution and schooling in America*. Teachers College Press.

Collins, P. H. (1990). *Black feminist thought: Knowledge, consciousness, and the politics of empowerment*. Routledge.

Costanza-Chock, S. (2020). *Design justice: Community-led practices to build the worlds we need*. The MIT Press.

Cross, N. (2001). Designerly ways of knowing: Design discipline versus design science. *Design Issues, 17*(3), 49–55.

Cuban, L. (1986). *Teachers and machines: The classroom use of technology since 1920*. Teachers College Press.

Davis, A. (2016). *Freedom is a constant struggle: Ferguson, Palestine, and the foundations of a movement*. Haymarket Books.

Della Porta, D. (2006). *Globalization from below: Transnational activists and protest networks*. University of Minnesota Press.

DeVos, B. (2015, March 11). Competition, creativity, and choice in the classroom. *SXSW Education*. http://www.federationforchildren.org/wp-content/uploads/2015/03/Betsy-SXSWedu-speech-final-remarks.pdf

Dickey, M.R. (2020, September 21). Twitter and Zoom's algorithmic bias issues. *Techcrunch*. Retrieved from: https://techcrunch.com/2020/09/21/twitter-and-zoom-algorithmic-bias-issues/.

Dixon-Román, E., Nichols, T. P., & Nyame-Mensah, A., (2020). The racializing forces of/in AI educational technologies. *Learning, Media, and Technology, 45*(3), 236–250.

Drucker, J. (2013). Reading interface. *PMLA, 128*(1), 213–220.

Duncan, A. (2010, November 17). The new normal: Doing more with less. *AEI*. https://www.aei.org/research-products/speech/the-new-normal-doing-more-with-less/

Durkheim, E. (1925/1961). *Moral education: A study in the theory and practice of the sociology of education*. Free Press.

Edgerton, D. (1999). From innovation to use: Ten eclectic theses on the historiography of technology. *History and Technology, 16*(2), 111–136.

Edwards, P., Jackson, S., Bowker, G., & Williams, R. (2009). An agenda for infrastructure studies. *Journal of the Association for Information Systems, 10*(5), 365–374.

Eubanks, V. (2018). *Automating inequality: How high-tech tools profile, police, and punish the poor.* St. Martin's Press.

Ewing, E. (2018). *Ghosts in the schoolyard: Racism and school closings on Chicago's South Side.* University of Chicago Press.

Fallace, T. D. (2015). *Race and the origins of progressive education, 1880–1929.* Teachers College Press.

Flores, N., & García, O. (2017). A critical review of bilingual education in the United States: From basements and pride to boutiques and profit. *Annual Review of Applied Linguistics, 37,* 14–29.

Foucault, M. (1977). *Discipline and punish: The birth of the prison.* Pantheon Books.

Freeman, C. (1982). *The economics of industrial innovation.* Pinter.

Garcia, A., & Nichols, T. P. (2021). Digital platforms aren't mere tools—they're complex environments. *Phi Delta Kappan, 102*(6), 14–19.

Gardner, H., & Davis, K. (2014). *The app generation: How today's youth navigate identity, intimacy, and imagination in a digital world.* Yale University Press.

Ghiso, M. P., Campano, G., & Simon, R. (2013). Grassroots inquiry: Reconsidering the location of innovation. *Language Arts, 91*(2), 105–112.

Godin, B. (2006). The linear model of innovation: The historical construction of an analytic framework. *Science, Technology, & Human Values, 31*(6), 639–667.

Gordon, R. (2016). *The rise and fall of American growth.* Princeton University Press.

Graham, S. & Perin, D. (2007). A meta-analysis of writing instruction for adolescent students. *Journal of Educational Psychology, 99,* 445–476.

Grubb, W.N., & Lazerson, M. (2004). *The education gospel: The economic power of schooling.* Harvard University Press.

Gunter, G., Rowlands, I., & Nicholas, D. (2009). *The Google generation: Are ICT innovations changing information-seeking behavior?* Chandos Publishing.

Harding, S. (2008). *Sciences from below: Feminisms, postcolonialities, modernities.* Duke University Press.

Hayman, S., & Coleman, J. (2016). *Parents and digital technology: How to raise the connected generation.* Routledge.

Herold, B. (2013). Philadelphia seeks salvation in lessons from model school. *Education Week.* Retrieved from: https://www.edweek.org/policy-politics/philadelphia-seeks-salvation-in-lessons-from-model-school/2013/09.

Hull, G. (2003). Youth culture and digital media: New literacies for new times. *Research in the Teaching of English, 38*(2), 229–233.

Jackson, P. (1968). *Life in classrooms.* Holt, Rinehart, & Winston.

Jackson, S. J., Edwards, P. N., Bowker, G., & Knobel, C. (2007). Understanding infrastructure: History, heuristics, and cyberinfrastructure policy. *First Monday, 12*(4), 1–10.

Jasanof, S., Markle, G., Petersen, J., & Pinch, T. (1995). *The handbook of science and technology studies.* Sage Publications.

Jenkins, H. (with Purushotma, R., Weigel, M., Clinton, K., & Robison, A. J.). (2006). *Confronting the challenges of participatory culture: Media education for the 21st century.* The MIT Press.

Johnson, D. (2000). W. E. B. Du Bois, Thomas Jesse Jones, and the struggle for social education, 1900–1930. *The Journal of Negro History, 85*(3), 71–95.

Jones, K., Robinson, C., & Vaughan, K. (2015). Deschooling, homeschooling, and unschooling in the alternative school milieu. In M. He, B. Schultz, & W. Schubert (Eds.), *The SAGE guide to curriculum in education* (pp. 391–399). Sage Publications.

Juliani, A.J. (2014). *Inquiry and innovation: Using 20% time, genius hour, and PBL to drive student success.* Eye on Education.

Jurow, S., Horn, I., & Philip, T. (2019). Re-mediating knowledge infrastructures: A site for innovation in teacher education. *Journal of Education for Teaching, 45*(1), 82–96.

Kafai, Y., Fields, D., & Searle, K. (2014). Electronic textiles as disruptive designs: supporting and challenging maker activities in schools. *Harvard Educational Review, 84*(4), 532–556.

Kafai, Y., Jayathirtha, G., Shaw, M., & Morales-Navarro, L. (2021). Codequilt: Designing an hour of code activity for creative and critical engagement with computing. In *Interaction Design and Children,* 573–576.

Kleinman, D. L. (1995). *Politics on the endless frontier: Postwar research policy in the United States.* Duke University Press.

Ladson-Billings, G. (2006). From the achievement gap to the education debt: Understanding achievement in U.S. schools. *Educational Researcher, 35*(7), 3–12.

Lankshear, C., & Knobel, M. (2011). *New literacies: Everyday practices and social learning.* McGraw-Hill.

Latour, B. (1987). *Science in action.* Harvard University Press.

Lessig, L. (2008). *Remix: Making art and commerce thrive in the hybrid economy.* Penguin.

Lewis, E. C. (2010). Friending Atticus Finch: English teachers' perspectives on MySpace as a contemporary framework for literary analysis. *Journal of Adolescent and Adult Literacy, 55*(4), 285–295.

Light, J. S. (2003). *From warfare to welfare: Defense intellectuals and urban problems in Cold War America.* Johns Hopkins University Press.

Litts, B., Searle, K., Brayboy, B., & Kafai, Y. (2021). Computing for all? Examining critical biases in computational learning tools. *British Journal of Educational Technology, 52*(2), 842–857.

Manzini, E. (2015). *Design when everybody designs: An introduction to design for social innovation.* The MIT Press.

Marsh, J., Arnseth, H.C., & Kumpulainen, K. (2018). Maker literacies and maker citizenship in the MakEY (Makerspaces in the Early Years) Project. *Multimodal Technologies and Interaction, 2*(3), 1–19.

Martin, R. (2003). *The organizational complex: Architecture, media, and corporate space.* The MIT Press.

Marvin, C. (1983). *When old technologies were new.* Oxford University Press.

Mattern, S. (2014). Library as infrastructure. *Places Journal.* https://placesjournal.org/article/library-as-infrastructure.

McLean, C.A., & Rowsell, J. (2021). *Maker literacies and maker identities in the digital age: Learning and playing through modes and media.* Routledge.

Murray, D (1972). Teach writing as a process not product. *The Leaflet, 71,* 11–14.

National Writing Project (2013, July). *Writers at work: Making and connected learning—A connected learning TV webinar series.* https://archive.nwp.org/cs/public/print/resource/4139

Neff, G. (2012). *Venture labor: Work and the burden of risk in innovative industries.* The MIT Press.

Nichols, T. P. (2020). Innovation from below: Infrastructure, design, and equity in literacy classroom makerspaces. *Research in the Teaching of English, 55*(1), 56–81.

Nichols, T. P. (2021). Innovating from the ground up. *Educational Leadership,* 33–37.

Nichols, T. P., & Coleman, J. J. (2021). Feeling worlds: Affective imaginaries and the making of democratic literacy classrooms. *Reading Research Quarterly, 56*(2), 315–335.

Nichols, T. P., & Johnston, K. (2020). Rethinking availability in multimodal composing: Frictions in digital design. *Journal of Adolescent and Adult Literacy, 64*(3), 259–270.

Nichols, T. P., & LeBlanc, R. J. (2020). Beyond apps: Digital literacies in a platform society. *The Reading Teacher, 74*(1), 103–109.

Nichols, T. P., LeBlanc, R. J. & Slomp, D. (2021). Writing machines: Formative assessment in the age of big data. *Journal of Adolescent and Adult Literacy, 64*(6), 712–719.

Nichols, T. P., & Lui, D. (2019). Learning by doing: The tenuous alliance of the maker movement and education reform. In J. Hunsinger and A. Schrock (Eds.), *Making our world: The hacker and maker movements in context* (pp. 1–20). Peter Lang.

Nichols, T. P., McGeehan, C., & Reed, S. (2019). Composing proximity: Teaching strategic distance to high school writers. *English Journal, 108*(3), 67–73.

Nichols, T. P., & Monea, B. (2019). Virtual "stuff": Digital pedagogies as a material practice. Paper presented at the Literacy Research Association. Tampa, FL.

Noble, S. (2018). *Algorithms of oppression: How search engines reinforce racism.* New York University Press.

Papert, S. (1993). *The children's machine: Rethinking school in the age of the computer.* Basic Books.

Paris, D. (2019). Naming beyond the white settler colonial gaze in educational research. *International Journal of Qualitative Studies in Education, 32*(3), 217–224.

Penuel, B. (2019). Infrastructuring as a practice of design-based research for supporting and studying equitable implementation and sustainability of innovations. *Journal of the Learning Sciences, 28*(4–5), 659–677.

Peppler, P., Halverson, E., & Kafai, Y. (2016). *Makeology: Makerspaces as learning environments.* Routledge.

Perrotta, C. (2020). Programming the platform university: Learning analytics and predictive infrastructures in higher education. *Research in Education, 109*(1), 53–71.

Piketty, T. (2014). *Capital in the 21st century.* Harvard University Press.

Plummer, E. C., Stornaiuolo, A., Li, G-G-S., Lott, J., Marrero, C. L., McLaine, D. Z., et al. (2020). Participatory ethnography: Developing a high school writing center in partnership. *Perspectives on Urban Education, 16*(1), 1–8.

Postman, N. (1992). *Technopoly: The surrender of culture to technology.* Vintage.

Prensky, M. (2010). *Teaching digital natives: Partnering for real learning.* Corwin.

Rittel, H. W. J., & Webber, M. M. (1973). Dilemmas in a general theory of planning. *Policy Sciences, 4*(2), 155–169.

Robinson, K. (2006). Do school's kill creativity? TED Talks. Retrieved from: https://www.ted.com/talks/sir_ken_robinson_do_schools_kill_creativity?language=en.

Rodney, W. (1972). *How Europe underdeveloped Africa*. Bogle-L'Ouverture Publicatons.

Rolph, A. (2017, April 3). This high school wants to revolutionize learning with technology. *USA Today*. https://www.usatoday.com/story/sponsor-story/xq/2017/04/03/high-school-wants-revolutionize-learning-technology/99985812/

Salisbury, K., & Nichols, T. P. (2020). School makerspaces: Beyond the hype. *Phi Delta Kappan, 101(8)*, 49–53.

Schneider, J. (2014). *From the ivory tower to the schoolhouse: How scholarship becomes common knowledge in education*. Harvard Education Press.

Schneider, J. (2015, October 10). American schools are modeled after factories and treat students like widgets. Right? Wrong. *The Washington Post*. https://www.washingtonpost.com/news/answer-sheet/wp/2015/10/10/american-schools-are-modeled-after-factories-and-treat-students-like-widgets-right-wrong/

Schneider, J., & Berkshire, J. (2020). *A wolf at the schoolhouse door: The dismantling of public education and the future of school*. The New Press.

Schumpeter, J. (1939). *Business cycles: A theoretical, historical, and statistical analysis of the capitalist process*. McGraw Hill.

Shapin, S., & Schaffer, S. (1985). *Leviathan and the air pump: Hobbes, Boyle, and the experimental life*. Princton University Press.

Smith, M. R., & Marx, L. (1994). *Does technology drive history? The dilemma of technological determinism*. MIT Press.

Star, S. L. (1999). The ethnography of infrastructure. *American Behavioral Scientist, 43*, 377–391.

Star, S. L., & Ruhleder, K. (1996). Steps toward an ecology of infrastructure: Design and access for large information spaces. *Information Systems Research, 7(1)*, 111–134.

Stornaiuolo, A., & Nichols, T. P. (2018). Making publics: Mobilizing audiences in high school makerspaces. *Teachers College Press, 120(8)*, 1–22.

Stornaiuolo, A., & Nichols, T. P. (2020). Makerspaces in K–12 schools: Six key tensions. In C.A. McLean & J. Rowsell (Eds.), *Maker literacies and maker identities in the digital age* (pp. 117–132). Routledge.

Stornaiuolo, A., Nichols, T. P., & Vasudevan, V. (2018). Building spaces for literacy in school: Mapping the emergence of a literacy makerspace. *English Teaching: Practice and Critique, 17(4)*, 357–370.

Strange, L. S., & Brown, R. S. (2002). The bicycle, women's rights, and Elizabeth Cady Stanton. *Women's Studies, 31(5)*, 609–626.

Taplin, J. (2017). *Move fast and break things: How Facebook, Google, and Amazon cornered culture and undermined democracy*. Little Brown.

Taylor, A. (2019). *Democracy may not exist, but we'll miss it when it's gone*. Metropolitan Books.

Taylor, C. (2003). *Modern social imaginaries*. Duke University Press.

Taylor, C. (2007). *A secular age*. Harvard University Press.

Taylor, K.-Y. (2016). *From #blacklivesmatter to Black liberation*. Haymarket Books.

Tuck, E. (2009). Suspending damage: A letter to communities. *Harvard Educational Review, 79(3)*, 409–428.

Turkle, S. (2017). *Alone together: Why we expect more from technology and less from each other.* Basic Books.

Turner, F. (2013). *The democratic surround: Multimedia and American liberalism from World War II to the psychedelic sixties.* University of Chicago Press.

Twenge, J. M. (2017). Have smartphones destroyed a generation? *The Atlantic.* https://www.theatlantic.com/magazine/archive/2017/09/has-the-smartphone -destroyed-a-generation/534198/

Twenge, J. M. (2018). *iGen: Why today's super-connected kids are growing up less rebellious, more tolerant, less happy—and completely unprepared for adulthood—and what that means for the rest of us.* Atria Books.

Tyack, D. B., & Cuban, L. (1995). *Tinkering toward Utopia: A century of public school reform.* Harvard University Press.

Urban, W. (2010). *More than science and Sputnik: The National Defense Education Act of 1958.* University of Alabama Press.

Utterback, J.M. (1974). Innovation in industry and the diffusion of technology. *Science, 183*(4124), 620–626.

Vallance, E. (1986). A second look at "conflicting conceptions of curriculum." *Theory into Practice, 25*(1), 24–30.

van Dijck, J. (2020). Seeing the forest for the trees: Visualizing platformization and its governance. *New Media & Society.* DOI: 10.1177/1461444820940293

Washington, H. A. (2008). *Medical apartheid: The dark history of medical experimentation on Black Americans from colonial times to the present.* Anchor.

Watters, A. (2015, April 25). The invented history of "the factory model of education." *Hack Education.* http://hackeducation.com/2015/04/25/factory-model

Watters, A. (2021). *Teaching machines: The history of personalized learning.* The MIT Press.

Weller, C. (2017, October 24). Bill Gates and Steve Jobs raised their kids tech-free— and it should've been a red flag. *The Independent.* https://www.independent.co .uk/life-style/gadgets-and-tech/bill-gates-and-steve-jobs-raised-their-kids-tech -free-and-it-should-ve-been-red-flag-a8017136.html

Wettrick, D. (2014). *Pure genius: Building a culture of innovation and taking 20% time to the next level.* Dave Burgess Consulting, Inc.

Whitney, A., & Friedrich, L. (2013). Orientation for the teaching of writing: A legacy of the National Writing Project. *Teachers College Record, 115*(7), 1–37.

Wiggins, G., & McTighe, J. (1998). *Understanding by design.* Association for Supervision and Curriculum Development.

Wigley, R. (2021). *Born digital: The story of a distracted generation.* Whitefox Publishing.

Williamson, B. (2020). Education technology seizes a pandemic opening. *Current History, 120*(822), 15–20.

Wolf, M. (2018, August 25). Skim reading is the new normal. The effect on society is profound. *The Guardian.* https://www.theguardian.com/commentisfree/2018 /aug/25/skim-reading-new-normal-maryanne-wolf

Index

About the Author

T. Philip Nichols is an assistant professor of Curriculum and Instruction at Baylor University and a former secondary school teacher. He studies how science and technology condition the ways we practice and talk about teaching, learning, and leadership, and the implications for equitable public education. His work has appeared in *Educational Researcher, Teachers College Record, Educational Leadership, Phi Delta Kappan*, and a range of other research and practitioner journals, as well as magazines like *The Atlantic* and *Logic*. He holds a PhD in Literacy, Culture, and International Education from the University of Pennsylvania, where he also earned an M.A. in History and Sociology of Science. He lives in Austin, TX.

Printed and bound by CPI Group (UK) Ltd, Croydon, CR0 4YY

09/06/2025

14685979-0001